D1029280

BOOKS BY **RANDALL KENNEDY**

Say It Loud!:
On Race, Law, History, and Culture

For Discrimination:
Race, Affirmative Action, and the Law

The Persistence of the Color Line:
Racial Politics and the Obama Presidency

Sellout:
The Politics of Racial Betrayal

Interracial Intimacies:
Sex, Marriage, Identity, and Adoption

Nigger:
The Strange Career of a Troublesome Word

Race, Crime, and the Law

NIGGER

The Strange Career of
a Troublesome Word

NIGGER

The Strange Career of
a Troublesome Word

RANDALL KENNEDY

With a New Introduction by the Author

Pantheon Books, New York

All rights reserved. Published in the United States by Pantheon
Books, a division of Penguin Random House LLC., New York,
and distributed in Canada by Penguin Random House Canada
Limited, Toronto. Originally published in hardcover in the
United States by Pantheon Books, a division of Penguin Random
House LLC., New York, in 2002, and subsequently in paperback,
in different form, by Vintage Books, a division of
Penguin Random House LLC, New York, in 2003.

Pantheon Books and colophon are registered trademarks of
Penguin Random House LLC.

Library of Congress Cataloging-in-Publication Data
Kennedy, Randall, [date]
Nigger / Randall Kennedy.
p.   cm.
Includes bibliographical references and index.
HC ISBN: 978-0-593-31652-8. EBK ISBN: 978-0-593-31675-7
1. United States—Race relations—Psychological aspects.
2. African Americans—Social conditions.   3. African
Americans—Race identity.   4. Racism in language.
5. Racism—United States—Psychological aspects.
6. English language—United States—Slang—Social aspects.
7. English language—United States—Slang—Psychological aspects.
8. Invective—United States—Psychological aspects.
9. Invective—United States—History—Anecdotes.   I. Title.
E185.625 .K46 2002 305.896'073—dc21 2001036442

www.pantheonbooks.com

Jacket design by Tré Seals
Book design by Johanna S. Roebas

Printed in the United States of America
Revised Edition, 2022
2 4 6 8 9 7 5 3 1

THIS BOOK IS DEDICATED TO

The Board

Gary E. Bell, Chairman for Life
Thaddeus J. Bell
Reginald S. Bell
Veta T. Bell Faison
William Hopkins
Henry H. Kennedy Jr.
Angela S. Kennedy Acree
Randall L. Kennedy
James L. Price Jr.
Clement A. Price
Jarmila L. Price
Cyril O. "Butch" Spann Jr.

This book is also dedicated to the parents of all the board members.
Special recognition is given to Anna Spann Price, Hattie Lillian Spann
Bell, and Rachel Spann Kennedy, the surviving daughters of Sellers Spann
and Lillian V. Spann (Big Mama). These three extraordinary women
have generously offered guidance, support, discipline, wisdom,
and love to all the members of The Board.

CONTENTS

to the Twentieth-Anniversary Edition

When *Nigger: The Strange Career of a Troublesome Word* was initially published twenty years ago, I predicted that the infamous N-word would survive efforts to bury it. Experience has sustained that prediction. *Nigger* remains a key word: dangerous, vital, evocative, volatile, unsettling, chameleonlike. Notorious the world over, it occupies a singular niche. No word comes close to generating the amount of controversy that *nigger* provokes.

The Strange Career of a Troublesome Word details the etymology of *nigger,* describes its deployment as a term of abuse, insult, and threat, notes ways in which dissidents have sought to put it to very different uses, and assesses mistakes people have made in attempting to erase from our culture the term that one lawyer famously branded "the filthiest, dirtiest, nastiest word in the English language."*

Here, with the benefit of a two-decade retrospective, I underline three points. The first is that, alas, *nigger* used conventionally—namely as an insult—continues to be an oft-heard feature of the soundtrack of American racism at its most base and violent. Any serious discussion of the N-word and proper ways to respond to its various uses must include an appreciation of the persistent weaponization of *nigger* by racists. The second point is that certain efforts to expunge *nigger* have gone awry, lost perspective, abandoned essential norms of freedom of thought and expression, and degenerated into petty tyranny. These are efforts to eradicate *nigger* categorically, or at least to make it verboten to whites no matter the context. The third point is a reiteration of my former prediction: *nigger* is here to stay, for bad and for good. For bad because certain uses of the word signify the presence of racism, often of a frighteningly violent sort. For good because other uses of the word—the presence of the word as a tool of antiracist protest, or as a comedic intervention, or as a gesture of solidarity, or as a sly term of endearment—manifest a wonderful capacity to transmute ugliness into art.

---

*That lawyer was Christopher Darden, who prosecuted O. J. Simpson for murder. He made this statement as part of an argument for withholding from the jury evidence that a key prosecution witness, Detective Mark Fuhrman, had not only referred to blacks as niggers but also lied under oath in denying the accusation. See Jeffrey Toobin, *The Run of His Life: The People v. O. J. Simpson* (1996).

1

Court opinions provide numerous examples of *nigger* used derisively, tauntingly, and threateningly. The word is found in the mouth of a convicted murderer who killed a woman and raped her fourteen-year-old sister in retaliation against the woman's romance with a "nigger."[1] It emerges in testimony in the civil rights prosecution of white police officers who beat two men of color who were accompanying white women to a party: "Nigger, shut up, it's our world."[2] It surfaces at the trial of a man who, because of racial animus, stabbed to death a teenager.[3] It attended the ramblings of an inmate who threatened a judge while mocking the tragic murder of the judge's mother and husband. Already serving a life term for murder, he sent the judge a letter that accused her of being a "race traitor and a Jude lover whore who prostitutes herself to the niggers, spics and Judes."[4] It festooned the statements of a white supremacist convicted of violating the Fair Housing Act. Mocking Martin Luther King Jr., the man said that his own dream was that all "niggers" would die.[5] It figures in the conduct of a university graduate student arrested for plastering on automobile bumpers an unwelcome sticker: "Racism is a horrible disease. You catch it from niggers."[6]

Civil litigation, too, uncovers numerous instances in which *nigger* is deployed for dastardly purposes. The most prevalent scenario is the employment discrimination lawsuit in which a black plaintiff accuses an employer of subjecting him to adverse treatment on account of race or consigning him to a racially hostile workplace. In the latter category of decided cases one frequently encounters the observation that "perhaps no single act can more quickly 'alter the conditions of employment and create an abusive working environment' than the use of an unambiguously racial epithet such as 'nigger' by a supervisor in the presence of his subordinates."[7]

Sometimes plaintiffs in discrimination or harassment suits prevail and win hefty damage awards. A black police officer in Saginaw, Michigan, was fired in retaliation for complaining about a fellow officer who referred to blacks as "niggers." Invoking federal and state antidiscrimination laws, a jury awarded him $1 million in damages.[8] Often, though, plaintiffs discover that litigation is a fickle enterprise surrounded by booby traps. Consider the situation of eleven black employees who worked at a warehouse where they were forced to endure an

> ongoing repetition of highly offensive racial insults—including the words "nigger," "Buckwheat," "boy," "monkey," and variations on these offensive racial pejoratives—spanning several decades and manifested in several different forms, including verbal insults, written graffiti, insulting caricatures, musical lyrics, and jokes. Much of this conduct occurred in public areas of the warehouse and was thus either actually seen by many employees or was likely seen by many employees. For example, an effigy was hung . . . with an accompanying

cardboard sign bearing an African-American supervisor's name and [the] words "nigger supervisor."[9]

When the aggrieved black employees sued, however, a federal district court judge granted summary judgment to the employer. The judge said that he found these incidents to be reprehensible. But he concluded that they were, as a matter of law, insufficiently severe or pervasive to constitute a hostile work environment. On appeal, one judge disagreed with the trial court, believing that the allegations, evidence, and law adduced by the plaintiffs entitled them at least to a trial. "The egregious facts in this record are sufficient," the judge averred, "to generate a dispute of material fact as to whether the Plaintiffs' work environment was hostile." That judge, however, was outvoted by two others who sided with the district court's dismissal of the lawsuit.[10]

This conclusion is not atypical. Viewing evidence too restrictively, many courts unwarrantedly dismiss abusive workplace lawsuits, determining that the conduct or conditions alleged are insufficiently awful to qualify as violations of the pertinent legislation.

An interesting subset of N-word cases features whites who, because of their commendable interventions, become victims of harassment. Tony Sayger was a white maintenance worker at a warehouse in Stuttgart, Arkansas. He heard his supervisor frequently refer to black workers in a racist fashion. This included, Sayger testified, "calling them 'niggers,' degrading their work, [and] saying they stunk." When Sayger objected and then recounted what he had heard in an internal investigation, he was laid off. Suing under federal and state laws, Sayger received a jury award of about $60,000.[11]

In other cases, whites have been victimized merely because of their associations with blacks. Scott Matusick was employed by the Erie County Water Authority in New York as a customer service representative, bill collector, and dispatcher. When it became known that he was dating a black woman (whom he later married), white colleagues began to harass him. On one occasion, according to Matusick, a supervisor put a pen to his neck and said, "You're a fucking nigger lover . . . your bitch is a . . . nigger, you're a fucking nigger now, too, and I'm going to kill all the fucking niggers." After being fired from his job, Matusick responded with a lawsuit in which he prevailed.[12]

Nigger as insult, *nigger* as taunt, *nigger* as signal of impending danger, remains a familiar presence. It is often said that the N-word is tabooed. The case law is full of statements by judges noting the peculiar noxiousness of the N-word as insult and asserting its status as a linguistic pariah. One court proclaimed the N-word to be "perhaps the most offensive and inflammatory racial slur in English."[13] But *nigger* as racist epithet remains in wide circulation. Sure, such usage is frowned upon in decent company. And it is sometimes subject, as we have seen, to legal sanction. Yet the racist use of *nigger* is by no means a rarity. And revelation that one has indulged in such usage is by no means necessarily a prelude to ostracism. When I wrote *The Strange Career of a Troublesome Word* twenty years ago, I alluded to a dustup provoked when the presidential candidate George W. Bush was overheard referring to a journalist as an "asshole." I asserted that, had he been caught referring to a journalist (or anyone else) as a "nigger," his candidacy would have been doomed because that usage, seen as a sign of unacceptable bigotry, would have been judged as disqualifying by a sufficiently large number of people.

There was a time, not so long ago, when that assertion seemed secure. In Wolfeboro, New Hampshire, the police commissioner Robert Copeland referred to President Obama as a "nigger" while talking with an acquaintance at a restaurant. Someone who overheard the remark complained to town authorities. Commissioner Copeland owned up to using the slur but refused to apologize.[14] A tide of denunciation engulfed him. The state's Republican U.S. senator demanded his resignation. So did the state's Democratic senator. So did the state's governor. So did numerous other local and national politicians. Copeland soon resigned. A similar fate overtook the Florida state senator Frank Artiles. He resigned amid an investigation of a private conversation in which he referred to certain colleagues as "niggers."[15]

I cannot confidently repeat my assertion now, in the cold shadow cast by the ascension of Donald Trump. Widely rumored to have a penchant for referring to blacks derogatorily as "niggers," Trump denied the accusation. Neither the accusation nor the denial, however, generated much of a stir. He benefited tremendously from having driven expectations about his conduct so low that some (like me) who abhor him and his politics and who believe the rumor about his linguistic predilections find themselves reduced to shrugging resignedly. We suspect that for many millions it would not matter, or matter much, if the rumor was substantiated by audiotapes like the "pussy grabbing" recordings.

One reason why the N-word occupies a large presence in the African American mind is that many—I venture to say most—black folk have a "nigger" story to tell: an episode in which they became the target of the N-word or overheard it used with racist derision. "There comes a time in the life of every African American," the sociologist Elijah Anderson remarks, "when he or she is powerfully reminded of his or her putative place as a black person." This is, he says, the "nigger moment," one liable to arise most anytime and anywhere, even in insulated settings.[16] Lawrence Graham chronicled such a moment, observing,

> I knew the day would come, but I didn't know how it would happen, where I would be, or how I would respond. It was the moment that every black fears: the day their child is called *nigger*.[17]

He then recounts how his fifteen-year-old son had called him from "a leafy New England boarding school" to report that two white men in a car had pulled up beside him as he walked and asked menacingly whether he was the only "nigger" at the school. According to Graham, school authorities minimized the racial import of the incident, saying that it was something that simply "just happens" in a place where town-gown relations are strained. He and his wife saw the episode as a much more threatening development. They felt it to be a blow that marked a sobering limitation in their ability to protect their children from prejudice.

The Grahams were right to be alarmed and angered because those men were clearly encroaching upon their son and using the N-word in an effort to upset or intimidate him. Assuming the accuracy of their perception that school authorities responded complacently, they were also right in insisting that those authorities be more invested in protecting members of their community against racist harassment. It is appropriate to condemn using the N-word intentionally to injure. It is appropriate, under carefully circumscribed circumstances, to view usage of the word as evidence of a crime, as when a jurisdiction distinctly punishes racially motivated violence or conduct undertaken with the specific intent of depriving a person of rights because of their race. It is appropriate to denounce any usage of the N-word that cannot be reasonably justified, taking into account the need to offer breathing room in assessing any and all communications. It is also appropriate to appeal to public opinion to repudiate unjustifiable usage of the N-word or any language used destructively.

Complacency in instances where condemnation is appropriate generates resentments that feed demand for censorship that is itself destructive. Apprehension that *nigger* as insult is far more prevalent and accepted than often recognized is part of what fuels eradicationist campaigns against the N-word. Displaced anger is thus vented, for example, upon white teachers who merely quote or mention *nigger* in lectures and classroom discussions. Mistaken outrage then narrows boundaries of intellectual, scholarly, and artistic freedom that should be widened.

2

Wayward responses to *nigger* have arisen in high schools, colleges, universities, and related settings. In Cambridge, Massachusetts, a high school teacher, Kevin Dua, directed students to pursue research on the history and effects of racial epithets. He called the project "Reclaiming: Nigger v. Cracker: Educating Racial Context in/for Cambridge." The students encountered difficulty insofar as computers at school blocked websites that might have been useful sources. To figure out a suitable way to address the problem, Dua scheduled a meeting to which students and school authorities were invited. Emily Dexter, a member of the Cambridge School Committee, which provides municipal oversight of the schools, attended the meeting, listened to the teacher's presentation, participated in discussion, and volunteered to assist the students with the problem posed by the computer filters. So far, so good. The situation presented a positive instance of public high school education in which teachers, students, and local political authorities gathered together around an exercise that sparked curiosity about an important subject.

But then things degenerated.

Some students became upset because Dexter, in one instance, enunciated the N-word in full. When Dexter heard that her remark had created hurt feelings, she returned to the high school to explain herself and apologize. But the teacher behind the project and some of the outraged students found Dexter's apology to be "insincere" and inadequate. Spurred by publicity, disquiet grew to such an extent that the Cambridge School Committee authorized a "fact finding review" of the incident. Subsequently, scores of principals, administrators, teachers, and coaches signed an open letter that demanded Dexter's resignation (which she eventually submitted). The letter warrants extended quotation because it conveys in tone and substance characteristic features found in many of the campaigns targeting "uses" of the N-word that are, by all accounts, nonracist in intention. The letter declared,

> The community members we serve need to know their school leaders have heard and understood their demands for aggressive steps to address racism in our schools. They need to see that all of us—including the members of our School Committee—are willing to accept responsibility for the failures that have led to this crisis.
>
> Regardless of your intent, we must all acknowledge that your use of the N-word, compounded by your botched apology to our students, has caused harm that cannot begin to be repaired while you remain in office.[18]

This letter is ridiculous. No one alleged that Dexter "used" the N-word to demean, harass, or terrorize. Perhaps there was a latent complaint that she negligently gave voice to what the

Boston Globe called "the full version of the N-word"[19] in a setting in which she should have anticipated that doing so would cause hurt feelings. But that charge, too, is mistaken. She was, after all, attending a meeting advertised as "Reclaiming: Nigger v. Cracker: Educating Racial Context in/for Cambridge." Why would anyone think that repeating a word in a title created by the convener of the meeting would be cause for complaint? Under the circumstances, it seems far-fetched to think that anyone would be troubled—or, more precisely, reasonably troubled—by merely enunciating an epithet under study. Throughout the controversy, Dexter demonstrated a desire to assist the teacher and the students with their project and sought repeatedly to clarify the intentions that had guided her choice of words—hardly the racist caricature created by her detractors.[20]

University life has also recently offered several examples of mistaken responses to *nigger* in situations where there was no predicate for sensible grievance. Consider what transpired at Augsburg University in Minneapolis. Professor Phillip Adamo assigned to a class James Baldwin's *Fire Next Time*. A student read out loud the following sentence: "You can only be destroyed by believing that you really are what the white world calls a *nigger*." Airing the N-word caused a commotion, as it had the previous year. Picking up on the anxiety and trying to use it productively, Professor Adamo instructed the students to ask themselves whether they believed that it was appropriate to voice the word. In posing the question, he repeated the word himself. A bit later he sent the class two essays on the politics of voicing the N-word. The next day stu-

dents asked Adamo to leave the classroom while they discussed the controversy among themselves. Adamo complied
with the request. His accommodation, however, did not quiet
the controversy; rather, it intensified. After a flurry of emails
in which Adamo tried to explain himself, university authorities removed him from the course and ousted him as the director of a prestigious program, all of which was prelude to
suspension and then early retirement.[21]

This farce reflected poorly on many people in the Augsburg
University community. The student complaint was foolish. As
Adamo stated in his own defense, there is "a distinction
between use and mention. To use the word to inflict . . . harm
is unacceptable. To mention the word in a discussion of how
the word is used is necessary for honest discourse."[22] This was
not a case of a professor calling someone "nigger." This was a
case of a professor exploring the thinking and expression of a
major writer who voiced the word to challenge racism.*

---

*Inattentiveness to this elementary distinction between "use" and "men-
tion" has led to dismaying consequences. Professor Adam Habib, director
of the University of London's School of Oriental and African Studies, was
suspended from his position—he has been reinstated—during the pen-
dency of an investigation into his "use" of the N-word. What had he done
to occasion suspicion? He spoke of the need to take action against any
member of the staff who used *nigger* against someone. That he enunciated
the word prompted some students to denounce him. For some of his
detractors, the problem involved more than his word choice; it also
involved Habib's identity as a person of Indian descent—as opposed to a
person of African descent—who had been born in South Africa and had
lived most of his life there. "You are not a black man," one of the students
declared, "you cannot use the word, regardless of your lived experience."
The student union issued a statement maintaining that Habib's comments

The case also reflected poorly on Adamo. Although he did nothing wrong initially, he compromised himself badly when he permitted himself to be cowed by the students. He probably should have refused the initial request to leave the classroom. But what came later was worse. In a letter to the class, he wrote that the classroom "is a place where any and every topic can be explored, even those topics considered to be taboo. This is how I understand academic freedom, which is a precious thing to me and other professors. It is the currency that allows us to speak truth to power." So far, so good. But in the next breath, Adamo stumbled into retreat: "I am now struggling to understand how it may be better not to explore some taboo topics, and to weigh the consequences of absolute academic freedom versus outcomes that lead to hurt, racial trauma, and loss of trust."[23] There is nothing wrong with repu-

---

were "unacceptable, disgusting, and to be unequivocally rejected." Rejecting calls that he step down from his position as director, Habib declared, "I am not sure why I should resign. No malevolent intention was behind my mention of the word. If anything, it was the opposite: a commitment to act if the word was used against another human being by anyone within our institutional community."

See Tobi Thomas, "Soas Students Call for Director to Resign over Use of N-Word," *Guardian,* March 12, 2021; "Adam Habib Steps Aside as N-Word Investigation Gets Under Way," *TimesLive,* March 18, 2021; Shonisani Tshikalange, "Adam Habib 'Is Not Racist' and Will Return to Work Next Week," *TimesLive,* May 5, 2021.

In another episode, a black security guard at a school was fired (though later reinstated) pursuant to a zero-tolerance N-word policy when he told a student to refrain from calling him a "nigger." See Madeleine Carlisle, "Black Security Guard Fired for Repeating the N-Word When Telling a Student Not to Call It to Get His Job Back," *Time,* October 22, 2019.

diating a position if there is good reason to do so. Adamo's abdication of his initial choice and the values surrounding it, however, was unwarranted (and thus, unsurprisingly, poorly explained). He had done nothing wrong, should have said so loudly, and should have held firm.

Several of Adamo's professional peers joined together in condemning him. They wrote an open letter to the university community that illustrates the anti-intellectualism, illiberal conformity, and taste for coercion that attend many of the recent N-word controversies on campus. "We believe," they wrote, "that further conversations about academic freedom can only take place after we acknowledge that harm has been done to these students." In other words, discussion of a central pillar of the university enterprise—academic freedom—must be put on hold until everyone agrees to the highly contestable claim that "harm" has been done by vocalizing the words of an esteemed author. Further, they urged the university to "require meaningful and challenging diversity, equity, and justice training for all faculty."*[24] One wonders whether the cate-

---

*The letter declares revealingly, "We the undersigned Augsburg faculty acknowledge that Professor Phil Adamo's repeated use of the N-word has caused harm to our students. This term, the most violent and racially charged word in American culture, has historically been used in the U.S. by white people to dehumanize and humiliate Black people. We also acknowledge that this harm was intensified when Adamo defended his use of the N-word multiple times against the objections of students of color. . . . The incident illustrates the urgent need for many of our faculty to be more self-critical in their positions of power and racial (as well as gender and other forms of) privilege. Furthermore, it underscores the very real power of words to cause damage and trauma. We believe that fur-

chism they had in mind would include room for pluralism and debate alongside "training" for "diversity" and "inclusion."

The parties at Augsburg most responsible for undermining academic ideals, however, were its president, Paul C. Pribbenow, and its provost, Karen Kaivola. They were the ones who, punishing Adamo, permitted a perfectly sensible pedagogical decision to be turned into an academic "crime." They were the putative leaders who, in a moment of crisis, failed their campus miserably.[25]

James Baldwin was at the center of another university-level N-word controversy. The poet and novelist Laurie Sheck, a professor at the New School in New York City, assigned to a graduate creative writing class a Baldwin essay in which he complained that Americans have "modified or suppressed and lied about all the darker forces in our history." Baldwin championed attempting "an unflinching assessment of the record."[26] Against that backdrop, Sheck asked the students whether they had seen the acclaimed documentary about Baldwin, *I Am Not Your Negro*. She noted that in the interview from which the documentary's title was derived, Baldwin did not say, "I am not your Negro." He actually said—and she repeated it verbatim—"I am not your nigger." In response to an inquiry from a student regarding Sheck's statement, the administration of the New School initiated an "investigation" that lasted

---

ther conversations about academic freedom can only take place after we acknowledge that harm has been done to these students. . . . This moment requires us to consider the causes of not just this incident but other pedagogical failures around issues of diversity, inclusion, and equity."

for months and did not end until after considerable pressure was brought to bear on the university by, among other organizations, the Foundation for Individual Rights in Education. Ultimately, no formal action was taken against Sheck. In the interim, however, she had understandably retained a lawyer and shouldered a heavy burden of anxiety until she was "cleared."[27]

Here again there was no colorable case to be made that a professor had "used" the N-word in a racist fashion. The issue was whether the word could be spoken at all, regardless of the aims of the speaker and other features of the context surrounding the term's vocalization. The professor and her students were not encountering one another as strangers; they were collaborators in an academic venture discussing the propriety of bowdlerizing Baldwin's language while supposedly championing his insistence on realism and candor. Troubling is that the inquiry about the professor's conduct penetrated beyond an initial screening for frivolousness.

Law schools have also witnessed a slew of N-word controversies over the past several years. Examples include a professor quoting from a speech that served as evidence in a criminal prosecution that gave rise to a leading Supreme Court First Amendment precedent (*Brandenburg v. Ohio*), a professor constructing a hypothetical intended to display different levels of tortious liability, a professor referring to a redacted version of "n____" in an examination question involving employment discrimination, and a professor quoting language attributed to Patrick Henry in debate over the ratification of the Constitution. In some of these cases, administrators admonished the professors. In several, gangs of educators excoriated peers they depicted as clueless or careless or malevolent racist oafs. In others, professors were subjected to "investigations." In one, a professor was suspended from teaching, prompting him to sue the university.[28]

In my professional life as a law professor, I frequently quote material in which the N-word appears. I also say *nigger* in other contexts, in which, in my view, voicing it is called for pedagogically. I do not "use" the N-word in the sense in which "use" is rightly condemned. I do not bandy it about to taunt, threaten, demean, or insult anyone. But I do quote the N-word. And I also say it on my own to drive home important lessons. If that be "use," so be it. Words best known for their function as slurs (not only *nigger* but *coon, porch monkey, jiga-boo,* and many more, including *bitch, fag, tranny,* and *cunt*) are revealing signs that repay close attention. Race relations law is a subject that I teach regularly. Study of that subject will be impoverished to the extent that it skirts grappling directly with a word best known as an epithet which, more than any other, has symbolized racial oppression in America.*

Another reason for enunciating *nigger* as opposed to resorting to euphemism or omission has been persuasively championed by Professor Eugene Volokh, who rightly insists that law

---

*Ta-Nehisi Coates is correct in observing that "if you could choose one word to represent the centuries of bondage, the decades of terrorism, the long days of mass rape, the totality of white violence that birthed the black race in America, it would be 'nigger.' " "In Defense of a Loaded Word," *New York Times,* November 23, 2013.

schools ought to prepare students for stresses they are likely to encounter in law practice.[29] Some of those stresses come from demands for candor and accuracy in legal proceedings, from the gathering of evidence, to the writing of briefs, to the presentation of oral arguments, to the drafting of judicial opinions. Research mainly conducted by Professor Volokh found *nigger* quoted in more than ninety-five hundred opinions written since 2000 by a wide range of jurists. They could have covered up *nigger,* as some judges do. But they decided not to for, among other things, the sake of precision. Law students should be trained to conduct themselves appropriately in light of reasonable professional expectations.*

What about those who say that hearing or reading the word

---

*Lawyers ought not be inattentive to alternatives, including the wishes of those who prefer to erase or mute the N-word. But they should pursue the course that enables them best to advance their professional obligation under the circumstances. A good example is offered in a report to the National Football League on workplace problems filed by the distinguished litigator Theodore V. Wells Jr., a partner at the Paul, Weiss law firm. The report quotes *nigger* thirty-nine times. It notes, "We caution at the outset that the language we describe is extremely vulgar. We have not used euphemisms or toned down racist, sexually explicit, misogynistic or homophobic references. The actual words must speak for themselves, for they are crucial in understanding how the players and others interacted." See Paul, Weiss, Rifkind, Wharton & Garrison LLP, "Report to the National Football League Concerning Issues of Workplace Conduct at the Miami Dolphins," February 14, 2014, filed in *NFL Mgmt. Council v. NFL Players Ass'n,* 125 F.Supp. 3d 449 (S.D.N.Y. 2015). Quoted in Randall Kennedy and Eugene Volokh, "The New Taboo: Quoting Epithets in the Classroom and Beyond," *Capital University Law Review* 49, no. 1 (2021): 41n148.

nigger is so hurtful that it interferes with their ability to learn, and for that reason ought to be avoided? I have two sets of responses, one that takes the objection at face value and one that questions the claim of hurt.

My first response pertains to those who do, in fact, feel real distress upon hearing or seeing *nigger*. A student who encountered a redacted version of the N-word in a hypothetical on a law school examination reported feeling "incredibly upset" and beset by "heart palpitations."[30] The good news is that feelings of hurt, alarm, or humiliation are not unchangeable givens untouched and untouchable by the ways in which educators respond to them. Such feelings are subject to management. Educators should attempt to enable students to exercise control over feelings that, uncontrolled, will jeopardize their schooling and careers.

The more that schools validate the idea that in the situation under discussion feelings of hurt, alarm, or humiliation are justified, the tighter those feelings will be embraced, and the more there will be calls to harden linguistic taboos in deference to them. Educational policy should push in the opposite direction. It should propound the message that under the circumstances relevant here there is no good reason to feel hurt, alarmed, or humiliated. It should also propound the messages that people can and should be taught to deal calmly with any word. Law schools in particular should advance this message because an attorney unable to focus on legal chores on account of merely seeing or overhearing the infamous N-word is an inadequately prepared attorney—a lawyer who is as vulnerable as a surgeon who falls apart upon seeing or handling blood.* The proper response is not to avoid pedagogically useful applications of the slur. The proper response is to figure out ways of enabling students to manage distress so that they can proceed to learn the lessons on offer, thereby attaining knowledge and skills that will undergird their abilities to attain their aspirations.

Second, claimed feelings of hurt need to be questioned. Isn't it possible, indeed likely, that some of these claims are mere scripts that students have been taught to regurgitate or, relatedly, mere expedient allegations whose efficacy students have observed as administrators have naively or cravenly capitulated to them? I ask because, in many of the recent cases arising from campuses, it is difficult to discern how students could possibly have felt threatened or demeaned by the conduct of which they disapprove so strenuously. I ask as well in the hope of prompting others to be more questioning. Otherwise, educators pushed into becoming censors will continue to offer incentives to those who brandish the specter of trauma to further diminish vital academic, intellectual, and aesthetic capacities and freedoms.

There is yet another reason why some teachers have decided never to utter the N-word no matter what the cir-

---

*Cf. Jeannie Suk Gersen, "The Trouble with Teaching Rape Law," *New Yorker,* December 15, 2014. Responding to objections to teaching rape law because some students find it so upsetting, Professor Gersen asks, "Imagine a medical student who is training to be a surgeon but who fears that he'll become distressed if he sees or handles blood. What should his instructors do?" His instructors should figure out some way to assist the student in managing that distress so that he can proceed with his medical duties.

cumstances. They are determined to avoid the distraction entailed by having to defend their language. They believe that even if mentioning the N-word would be justifiable, the cost of explanation is prohibitive. Professors I admire have taken this position.* I respect their careful balancing even as I disagree with their conclusion. Pluralism requires such deference. I insist, however, that deference be shown as well to the professor who, for reasonable pedagogical purposes, chooses to enunciate the N-word.

In an overwhelming majority of the disputes noted above, the speaker criticized for "using" the N-word was white. That pattern is not accidental. Many participants in N-word controversies expressly demand an asymmetrical rule under which black speakers are given leeway while nonblack speakers are held to a clear, rigid, strictly enforced injunction: anyone other than blacks are forbidden under any circumstances to enunciate or spell out in full the notorious N-word. Some insist upon this discrimination in the strongest terms: according to the lawyer-journalist Elie Mystal, "I can say it, you can't, fuck you if that bothers you."[31]

Although that rule would privilege me as an African American, I abjure the "privilege." All persons should be equally free, regardless of attribution of identity, to use any language in a good faith effort to produce art or advance education. It is a dreadful betrayal of sound intellectual and artistic proce-

*See, e.g., Tom Bartlett, "A Professor Has Long Used a Racial Slur in Class to Teach Free-Speech Law. No More, He Says," *Chronicle of Higher Education,* March 7, 2019 (describing Professor Geoffrey Stone).

dure to erect identity-based boundaries with respect to who can say what. Race matching in the cultural domain—pairing writers or actors or translators with writings, roles, or subjects deemed appropriate to their ascribed identity—has a long history mainly characterized by the privileging of whites. Recently, though, race matching on behalf of racial minorities has been effectuated through programs of cultural reparations and protectionism.[32] With respect to our subject—the administration of the N-word—race matching entails blacks exercising monopoly over "use" of *nigger* while all others are made to stay clear of it.* Thus, the film director Spike Lee has declared that because of his racial status as a black man he has "more of a right" to deploy the N-word in filmmaking than a white director such as Quentin Tarantino.[33] Those in agreement with Lee's position have been unable to rigorously police that boundary line in film; Tarantino and other white filmmakers have continued to produce movies in which *nigger* has figured prominently. More successful have been efforts to police comedy. Scores of comedy routines are built around the conceit, which is also the reality, that no matter how fully a white comedian has ingratiated himself with black audiences,

---

*An example is Rebecca Carroll declaring in *Ebony* magazine, "As much as I hate the N-word, I do believe that it's Jay and Kanye's prerogative to use it—yes, because they are Black. But Gwyneth Kate Paltrow, you do not get to use that word in any context, ever. However authentic your friendships are with the Black folks in your life, these friendships do not provide you with the same perks as your American Express Black card. They do not buy you access to whatever hip aspect of Black culture appeals to you." Rebecca Carroll, "[MediaBOMB] Gwyneth Paltrow Use of N-Word Lost in Translation," *Ebony,* June 4, 2012.

the one thing that he absolutely cannot do on pain of repudiation and ostracism is say *nigger.* Black comedians can and do say *nigger,* but not white comedians.*

This dynamic erupted into view when the comedian Bill Maher got into trouble because of a quip he tossed off during his show *Real Time.* Interviewing the Republican U.S. senator Ben Sasse of Nebraska, Maher said at one point, facetiously, "I've got to get to Nebraska more." Sasse replied, "You're welcome. We'd love to have you work in the fields with us." Maher responded, "Work in the fields? Senator, I'm a house nigger." Soon thereafter the altogether predictable routine began. First, there were the expressions of indignation. DeRay Mckesson, an activist associated with Black Lives Matter, tweeted, "But really, @Bill Maher has got to go. There are no explanations that make this acceptable." The hip-hop star Chance the Rapper tweeted, "Please HBO Do Not Air Another Episode of Real Time with Bill Maher." Senator Sasse allowed as to how he wished that he'd had the presence of mind to admonish Maher immediately. After all, he declared, "the history of the

---

*There are always exceptions. The insult comedian Lisa Lampanelli caused a stir when she tweeted photos of herself and Lena Dunham with the caption "Me with my nigga @Lena Dunham of @HBOGirls—I love this beyotch." She was, predictably, lectured by disapproving observers who complained that she had crossed the race line in *nigger* usage. Lampanelli, however, remained unmoved, refusing to apologize or to alter her language. Her object of admiration, Lena Dunham, reacted differently. She tweeted, "That's not a word I would EVER use. . . . I was made supremely uncomfortable by it." See Eric Deggans, "Is It Ever OK for White People to Say the N-Word?," *Salon,* February 21, 2013; Shayla Pierce, "Why It's Never OK for White People (Including Lisa Lampanelli) to Use the N-Word," *XO Jane,* February 21, 2013.

N-word is an attack on universal human dignity. It's therefore an attack on the American Creed. Don't use it."[34] Professor Marc Lamont Hill averred that "white people should just never say that word. . . . No matter how down you think you are, you're still white and you can't use it."[35] On the show following the "house nigger" imbroglio, Maher set the stage for further denunciations, inviting onto his program entertainers and commentators who ritualistically chastised him. Maher's joke, the Democratic Party strategist Symone Sanders insisted, was "a slap in the face to black America." The N-word, Ice Cube asserted, has long been "used as a weapon by white people, and we're not gonna let it happen again. That's our word now. And you can't have it back."[36]

Second, there was the round of formulaic apologies. Home Box Office stated contritely, "Bill Maher's comment . . . was completely inexcusable and tasteless. We are removing his deeply offensive comment from any subsequent airings of the show." Next it was Maher's turn: "The word was offensive and I regret saying it and am very sorry."[37] Maher's apology, of course, was almost certainly insincere, the statement of a man who felt that he was a hostage and therefore entitled to tell the sorts of lies that hostages tell without fear of internal revulsion because, after all, they are speaking under duress. One might have hoped that Maher would refuse to engage in spurious apology. He holds himself out as a bold, freethinking critic-comedian. His capitulation, however, displayed the fear that even putative iconoclasts have of being caught on the wrong side of a dispute involving the N-word.

In a *New York Times* column, "Please Stop Apologizing," Maher had ridiculed the culture of complaint that prompts people to voice hurts and demand amends, even in circumstances in which no sensible observer could discern a basis for aggrievement. "Let's have an amnesty," he wrote, "on every made-up, fake, totally insincere, playacted hurt, insult, slight and affront."[38] Yet protests prompted him to apologize even though it was clear that he was deploying *nigger* ironically. He appears to have been overcome by the relentless pressure of Big Entertainment's commercial bottom line: living large exacts a hefty, freedom-diminishing price even for wealthy celebrities. It was sad to see Maher whipped into line so abjectly.

Although there is considerable momentum behind the demand for racial asymmetry in many social sectors, it is noteworthy that the little case law speaking to the issue favors a symmetrical rule. Consider the case of the white reporter for a Fox television station in Philadelphia who sued his employer after he was suspended and constructively discharged from his position for having "used" the N-word.[39] He enunciated the term in full in a meeting with a multiracial group of colleagues as they discussed how best to cover a story featuring a symbolic burial of the N-word by the National Association for the Advancement of Colored People (NAACP). The white reporter later explained that he "wanted to make the point that . . . if we're going to refer to the word 'nigger,' we should either say the word 'nigger' or refer to it as a racial epithet or a slur instead of using the phrase the 'N' word."[40] When the white reporter, in making his argument, said *nigger,* an African American colleague objected, exclaiming, "I can't believe you just said that!" According to a judge, "Nobody at the meeting believed that [the white reporter] used the word in its pejorative sense as a racial slur."[41] Still, rumors about the incident seeped out into the work site and beyond, garnering negative publicity, prompting disciplinary measures against the reporter, and eventually causing his departure from the station. The reporter, however, did not leave quietly. He maintained that in contrast to him three black colleagues who had said or written *nigger* were not disciplined. He recalled a newsroom editorial meeting at which he and his coworkers were discussing a "dumb criminal" story in which the perpetrator was an African American. A black journalist commented, "Man, that's one dumb nigger." According to the reporter, all of the attendees at the meeting laughed. The African American journalist received no penalty. But the white reporter did. According to him, his race—his whiteness—explained the disparate treatment: a difference in treatment that, he claimed, violated federal antidiscrimination law.[42]

The presiding judge was forced to confront a matter of first impression: "Can an employer be held liable under Title VII [of the Civil Rights Act of 1964] for enforcing or condoning the social norm that it is acceptable for African Americans to say 'nigger' but not whites?" The judge answered in the affirmative, opening up the possibility for the white reporter to prevail if he could convince a jury of the accuracy of his allegations. The judge conceded that "one can see how people in general, and African Americans in particular, might react differently when a white person uses the word than if an African American uses it." Still, he was "unable to conclude that this is a justifiable reason for permitting the Station to draw race-based distinctions between employees." In the judge's view, "It is no answer to say that we are interpreting Title VII in accord with prevailing social norms. Title VII was enacted to counter social norms that supported widespread discrimination against African Americans." The judge concluded that neither the text of Title VII, nor its legislative history, nor precedent suggested or permitted a departure from Title VII's command that employers refrain from "discriminating against any individual . . . because of such individual's race."[43]

Case law from a different direction also supports a symmetrical rule, appearing to be indifferent to the racial status of the speaker. Brandi Johnson, an African American woman, sued her employer, STRIVE, a social services organization, on account of her boss, Rob Carmona, whom a judge described as "a dark-skinned Puerto Rican male." Carmona repeatedly referred to Johnson as a "nigger" and admonished her to stop acting like a "nigger." At trial he maintained that he had used the N-word "out of love" to motivate Johnson. He claimed that in using *nigger,* he meant to convey to Johnson that she was "too emotional" and "too wrapped up in . . . the negative aspects of human nature." He argued that his rough language was aimed at helping her to succeed professionally. He and STRIVE denied that Johnson had been subjected to a racially hostile work environment or that the termination of her employment after her complaints had anything to do with illicit retaliation. The jury sided with Johnson, awarding her compensatory and punitive damages.[44]

Another successful black-on-black lawsuit was *Weatherly*

et al. v. Alabama State University, in which black female plaintiffs successfully sued a historically black college for subjecting them to a racially hostile workplace.[45] Their supervisors—a black man and a black woman—repeatedly used the N-word, remarking, "I'm tired of nigger shit," and referring to the university's mass transportation system as "the nigger bus line." Moreover, at least once a supervisor called one plaintiff's seven-year-old son "a nigger" in his presence, a comment that upset the child so much that he crawled under his mother's desk and curled up into a fetal position.[46] Rejecting the notion that black defendants should be given safe harbor, the jury sided with the plaintiffs, awarding them sizable recoveries.

Jurists interpreting antidiscrimination statutes are not the only ones demanding a symmetrical rule that avoids *racial* discrimination. Some arbiters of public opinion are doing so, too, pushing an eradicationist agenda full bore by insisting upon the muting or erasing of *nigger* altogether, regardless of the identity of the speaker or writer.[47] The columnist Jonathan Capehart writes, for example, that he wishes that everyone would have the good sense to avoid saying the N-word under any circumstances (though he neglects to explain why saying *N-word* itself is not a violation of his proposal).* Campaigns to comprehensively erase the N-word have led to efforts to bar it

---

*If *N-word* is permissible, what about *nigga* or some formulation other than N-I-G-G-E-R? Capehart, whose work I generally applaud, goes on to say that if a person ends up saying the word in a class for purposes of instruction, "I might be willing to give you a pass. But it would be better to pass on saying it at all." See Jonathan Capehart, "Should You Say the N-Word? No, Especially if You're Not Black," *Washington Post,* May 7, 2021.

as a word eligible for play in Scrabble competition.[48] Such efforts have also led to bowdlerizations. We saw this previously with the altering of Baldwin's language ("I am not your [Negro]"). A publisher has substituted *slave* for *nigger* in every appearance of the N-word in Mark Twain's *Adventures of Huckleberry Finn*.[49] Another publisher has edited the title of a Joseph Conrad novel, changing it from *The Nigger of the Narcissus* to (no kidding!) *The N-Word of the Narcissus*.[50]

3

I eschewed wholesale eradicationism twenty years ago and reject it now. One reason is prudential, a fear that people in a position to censor will do what people in positions of power often do: behave stupidly and with prejudice, giving vent to dictatorial impulses of the sort that have led to the punishment of conscientious teachers. So I want to restrict the power of arbiters of taste, particularly those armed with governmental authority. I want to inhibit their desire and ability to prohibit what people can say or hear, portray or see. I want to restrain them from banning or bowdlerizing or confining to a locked closet Cecil Brown's *Life and Loves of Mr. Jiveass Nigger*, Gil Scott-Heron's *Nigger Factory*, Carl Sandburg's "Nigger Lover," Carl Van Vechten's *Nigger Heaven*, Flannery O'Connor's "Artificial Nigger," Henry Dumas's "Double Nigger," Ed Bullins's *Electronic Nigger*, or Dick Gregory's *Nigger*—not to mention the many other stories, plays, novels, and other works that are constantly menaced because they contain the N-word.

But there is more to it than that. There are people of all backgrounds, including different racial identities, who put *nigger* to uses that are enjoyable, instructive, and moving. They do so in protest, satire, comedy, and all manner of gestures that are hard to characterize but richly expressive. I began this introduction detailing despicable uses to which *nigger* is put. I have not forgotten that horrific catalog. But neither can I forget the way in which commentators, activists, novelists, playwrights, comedians, and many ordinary folks have used *nigger* creatively to poke at racism, to signal solidarity with those wrongly demeaned, to communicate playfully and ironically with intimates, and to express all sorts of other sentiments.

My father, of blessed memory, an African American Louisianian born in 1917, used *nigger* often. He used it to compliment people, as when he said that of the "niggers" he had come across in his lifetime, Professor Allison Davis was the smartest, the Reverend James Hinton was the bravest, and the baseball star Jackie Robinson was the greatest. He used it as a friendly salutation: "Good to see you, my nigger." He used it to convey respect: "Thurgood Marshall is a stand-up nigger." Yes, he used the term to identify people of whom he disapproved: "Them niggers should be ashamed of themselves." But he also used it pridefully to refer to himself: "I am a stone nigger." My father used *nigger* frequently and without shame to convey a spectrum of beliefs and emotions that could be properly understood only by listening carefully to the intonation of his voice. In my childhood household, therefore, I learned about what the journalist Jarvis DeBerry referred to as the N-word's beautiful multiplicity of functions.[51] Of course, there are vestiges of childhood socialization that are best abandoned. But this lesson in the complexities and capacities of language is not one of them. To the contrary, it is a valuable lesson that deserves championing.

I am glad that I learned that *nigger*—like *any** symbol—is capable of being used to express contradictory emotions. And I am glad that that lesson has stuck with me. It has helped me to avoid susceptibility to the trauma alluded to as a reason for obsessively scrubbing the N-word wherever it emerges. And it has allowed me to appreciate teachings, creations, and performances that would be mangled if not wholly proscribed if *nigger* eradicationism prevailed. I enjoy the wordplay of August Wilson and Quentin Tarantino, though *nigger* is sprinkled liberally in the mouths of their characters. I delight in listening to "Still D.R.E." (Snoop Dogg and Dr. Dre) and "My Mind Playing Tricks on Me" (Geto Boys), though *nigger* is pervasive in the lyrics. I relish listening to the *nigger*-filled comedy routines of Dave Chappelle, Katt Williams, Chris Rock, and Richard Pryor, particularly new ways in which they deploy the N-word, as when some of them use it to refer to white people like Donald Trump. (I am well aware that later in his life Pryor repudiated his earlier playfulness with *nigger*. I believe, though, that the comedy that used *nigger*—the comedy exemplified in *That Nigger's Crazy*—was deeper, sharper, and funnier than his later work.)

Nigger remains a powerful weapon of disparagement, in-

---

*The swastika? The burning cross? Klan regalia? The Confederate flag? I stand by my claim with respect to all of them.

flicting contagious contempt. It continues to be wielded by some as an implement of bigotry. Deployed in a racist fashion, it still can and does draw psychic blood. But despite the abhorrent uses to which *nigger* is often put, seeking to ban it altogether is folly. The extent and intensity of the repression that would be required to obliterate *nigger* would impose costs that far outweigh any good that can be foreseen. Having to tolerate to some extent—even a large extent—obnoxious, even racist uses of *nigger* is, in my view, an acceptable price to pay for the freedom that a vigorous ethic of expressive pluralism demands and encourages. That is why I say anew that I hope that "*nigger* . . . is destined to remain with us . . . a reminder of the ironies and dilemmas, the tragedies and glories, of the American experience."[52]

INTRODUCTION

Nigger has accompanied me throughout my life. As a child growing up in Columbia, South Carolina, and Washington, D.C., in the '50s and '60s I assumed that *nigger* (along with various other racial slurs including *cracker* or *peckerwood*) would be in the minds, if not on the lips, of participants in any altercation pitting whites against blacks. I do not remember the first time that a white person called me "nigger," but I do remember the first time that responding to it gave rise to a discussion between me and my parents. The episode occurred in the early 1960s. After battling a white boy for what seemed like hours on a D.C. playground (at the Takoma Elementary School), I walked home and at dinner calmly related the events of the day. I asked my parents for advice on how best to react to a white person who called me "nigger." They gave me contradictory advice. My father said that I had standing permission from him to "go to war." He warned me against rushing into a fight if I was badly outnumbered. Otherwise, though, he urged me to respond with fists, or if necessary, with bottles, sticks, or bricks. My mother, on the other hand, recommended that I pay no heed to racial taunts, avoid bullies, and let bigots stew in their own poisonous prejudices. She insisted that while "sticks and stones may break your bones, words need never harm you."

Yet it was a word—this word *nigger*—that lay at the core of a recollection that revealed to me the pain my mother continues to feel on account of wounds inflicted upon her by racists during the era of Jim Crow segregation. Several years ago I asked her to tell me about her earliest memory of the color line. She began laughingly, telling me about how, in Columbia, she had often accompanied her mother to white folks' homes to pick up and return laundry. Although they typically traveled on public buses, my mother had failed to notice that her mother, Big Mama, always took her to the back of the bus where Negroes were segregated. One day, Big Mama asked my mother to run an errand that required her to catch a bus on which they had often ridden together. This errand marked the first time that my mother rode the bus on her own. She stood at the correct stop, got on the right bus, and deposited the appropriate fare. Being a bit scared, however, she sat down immediately behind the bus driver. After about a block, the driver pulled the bus over to the curb, cut the engine, and suddenly wheeled around and began to scream at my mother who was all of about eight or nine years old—"Nigger, you know better than to sit there! Get to the back where you belong!"

At this point in the storytelling, my mother was no longer laughing. A tear dropped onto her cheek, as she recalled running away from the bus overcome by fright.

I have been called "nigger" to my face on a couple of occasions by people who sought to convey their racial hatred or contempt for all blacks including me. In the spring of 1978, a motorist in Oxford, England, slowed down, rolled down the window of his car, and made a gesture indicating that he needed assistance. When I reached the side of his auto, he screamed "Nigger go home!" and sped off. Seven years later, on my first day in residence as a member of the faculty at Harvard Law School, a cabbie called me "nigger" (as well as "coon," and "jigaboo") on the basis of no apparent provocation other than my race.

I have also encountered *nigger* in dealings with acquaintances. Explaining why there were no blacks on a swimming team to which he belonged, a white elementary school classmate innocently allowed me access to familial information that I am sure his parents would have preferred for him to have kept private. My classmate told me that he had heard his parents and their friends say that they needed some "relief from niggers."

Years later, at a junior tennis tournament, I found myself sharing a hotel room with a white youngster from Mobile, Alabama. Late one evening, right as we were about to shut off the lights and go to sleep, this guy decided to tell me a final joke, one in which a reference to a "nigger" constituted the punch line. As soon as that line escaped his lips, his eyes bulged while the rest of his face froze. He knew immediately that he had made himself vulnerable to a judgment that he deeply feared. Why had he done so? I suspect that he had become so comfortable with me that he ceased, at least temporarily, to see me in terms of race. Or perhaps he had merely granted me the status of an honorary white. Either way, the reference to "nigger" seems to have suddenly made him aware anew of my blackness and thus the need to treat me differently than other acquaintances. I said nothing during the awkward silence that enveloped the room as his voice trailed away from the failed joke.

He apologized.

I do not recall whether or not I actually felt offended, but I do remember that from that moment on, the ease that had marked our budding friendship vanished.

For many people, saying or hearing *nigger* is easier in monoracial as opposed to multiracial settings. That has often been my experience. In my final year at my wonderful high school, St. Albans School for Boys, a black friend jokingly referred to me as a nigger in the presence of one of our white classmates. If he and I had been alone, I might have overlooked his comment or even laughed. But given the presence of the white classmate, I concluded immediately that a show of forceful disapproval was imperative. My concern was twofold and had to do in part with my position as student body president. I did not want the white classmate—and, through him, other white classmates—to get the impression that *nigger* was less injurious and more acceptable than what they had probably been taught at home. Aware of the ignorance of many of my white classmates regarding things racial, I regarded it as my duty to impress upon them the conventional wisdom which declared that *nigger* is an ugly, evil, irredeemable word. For reasons I will discuss below, my real beliefs regarding the N-word were more complicated but I thought that it would be impossible to relate those nuances to my white classmates. So I decided simply to condemn "nigger" wholesale. In addition, I believed that I had to come down as hard on my black classmate as I would have come down on a white classmate or else be subject to charges of hypocrisy, or even prejudice. So I sternly told my black classmate to refrain from referring to me by "that word" and that if he failed to restrain himself I would give him demerits that would force him to attend a disciplinary session at the school on a Saturday morning.

I think that my black classmate knew what I was thinking. But he was in no mood to go along. He laughed in my face, pointed at me, and with a raised voice cackled "nigger-nigger-nigger-nigger-nigger-nigger!" I immediately gave him a couple of hours of demerits and joined him on Saturday to make sure that he was present for his punishment.

Because of the way that *nigger* was used in my household I learned at an early age that it could be said in many ways, put to many uses, and mean many things. Big Mama peppered her speech with references to "niggers" by which she meant discreditable Negroes, a group that, in her view, constituted a large sector of the African American population. If Big Mama saw blacks misbehaving she would often roll her eyes, purse her lips, and then declare in a mournful tone, "Nigguhs!" According to Big Mama, "niggers can't get along, not even in church" and "are always late, even to their own funerals." She swore that she would never allow a "nigger doctor" to care for her and repeatedly warned that "if you see a bunch of niggers coming, turn around and go the other way."

Big Mama had clearly internalized antiblack prejudice. She truly believed that white people's water was wetter than black people's water, that as a rule, whites were nicer, better looking, and more capable than blacks. There was no affection or irony in her use of *nigger*. She deployed it exclusively for purposes of denigration. But life, of course, is complicated. This same Big Mama was a pillar of her all-black community in Columbia and a stalwart supporter of her children, grandchildren, and great-grandchildren—black folk who loved, indeed, idolized her. We recognized with sadness her antiblack prejudice but thoroughly rejected it as a consequence of competing influences, particularly the black college students who so magnificently spearheaded the southern struggle for emancipation from Jim Crow pigmentocracy.

As I attained maturity in the '60s and '70s, relatives and friends used *nigger* but in ways that differed substantially from Big Mama's usage. Some deployed it as a signal that they understood that blacks remained mere "niggers" in the eyes of many whites. For them, referring to blacks as niggers was a way of holding up a clarifying mirror to society and reminding all within earshot of what they saw as an unchanging reality of American life—"ofays on top, niggers on the bottom." Others used the term with a large twist of irony to speak admiringly of someone, as in "James Brown is a sho nuff nigger," meaning that the great entertainer was wholly willing to be himself without apology. If Big Mama said that a person had acted like a nigger, it could only mean that, in her view, someone had behaved badly. By contrast, when my cousins and their friends said that someone had acted like a nigger it might mean that that person had reacted to racist challenge with laudable militancy. Big Mama warned us about "bad niggers" by which she meant Negroes who were in trouble with the law. But among my cousins, as among many blacks, being a certain sort of "bad nigger"—the sort that bravely confronted the laws of white supremacy—was glamorous and admirable. Big Mama warned her charges against "acting like niggers." But a popular saying among the youngsters was "Never give up your right to act like a nigger," by which they meant that Negroes should be unafraid to speak up loudly and act out militantly on behalf of their interests.

There was often a generational difference in evidence in competing uses of the N-word with the younger people experimenting with nonderogatory versions. On the other hand, while some of my younger relatives are adamantly opposed to any use of *nigger,* believing it to be only and unalterably a debasing slur, some of my older relatives anticipated by many years the transformation of *nigger* (or "nigga") that is now widely attributed to the hip-hop culture. Long before the rapper Ice-T insisted upon being called a nigger, my father declared that he was proud to be a "stone nigger"—by which he meant a black man without pretensions who was unafraid to enjoy himself openly and loudly despite the objections of condescending whites or insecure blacks.

How could the man who gave me permission to "go to war" against racial insult turn around and proudly refer to himself as a nigger? My father could do so because he intuited what Justice Oliver Wendell Holmes once observed—that "a word is not a crystal, transparent and unchanged," but is instead "the skin of a living thought [that] may vary greatly in color and content according to the circumstances and time in which it is used."

I relate some of my own direct experiences with the N-word in response to questions I have received since the publication of *Nigger;* in the afterword to this edition I address still other questions and objections. Many people have asked whether or under what circumstances I have personally had to grapple with the word. For some questioners, my book is more authentic and acceptable insofar as I have been called a nigger and have otherwise been forced to encounter it in my own life. I make no such claim on my own behalf. I do not believe that my experiences entitle me to any more deference than that which is due on the strength of my writing alone. Experience is only an opportunity; what matters is what one makes of it. The extent to which my writing is appreciated or deferred to should be determined solely on the basis of *its* character. The best evidence of that is found on the page.

NIGGER

The Strange Career of
a Troublesome Word

CHAPTER ONE

The Protean N-Word

How should *nigger* be defined? Is it a part of the American cultural inheritance that warrants preservation? Why does *nigger* generate such powerful reactions? Is it a more hurtful racial epithet than insults such as *kike, wop, wetback, mick, chink,* and *gook*? Am I wrongfully offending the sensibilities of readers right now by spelling out *nigger* instead of using a euphemism such as *N-word*? Should blacks be able to use *nigger* in ways forbidden to others? Should the law view *nigger* as a provocation that reduces the culpability of a person who responds to it violently? Under what circumstances, if any, should a person be ousted from his or her job for saying "nigger"? What methods are useful for depriving *nigger* of destructiveness? In the pages that follow, I will pursue these and related questions. I will put a tracer on *nigger,* report on its use, and assess the controversies to which it gives rise. I have invested energy in this endeavor because *nigger* is a key word in the lexicon of race relations and thus an important term in American politics. To be ignorant of its meanings and effects is to make oneself vulnerable to all manner of perils, including the loss of a job, a reputation, a friend, even one's life.[1]

Let's turn first to etymology. *Nigger* is derived from the Latin word for the color black, *niger*.[2] According to the *Random House Historical Dictionary of American Slang,* it did not originate as a slur but took on a derogatory connotation over time. *Nigger* and other words related to it have been spelled in a variety of ways, including niggah, nigguh, niggur, and niggar. When John Rolfe recorded in his journal the first shipment of Africans to Virginia in 1619, he listed them as "negars." A 1689 inventory of an estate in Brooklyn, New York, made mention of an enslaved "niggor" boy. The seminal lexicographer Noah Webster referred to Negroes as "negers." (Currently some people insist upon distinguishing *nigger*—which they see as exclusively an insult—from *nigga,* which they view as a term capable of signaling friendly salutation.)[3] In the 1700s *niger* appeared in what the dictionary describes as "dignified argumentation" such as Samuel Sewall's denunciation of slavery, *The Selling of Joseph.* No one knows precisely when or how *niger* turned derisively into *nigger* and attained a pejorative meaning.[4] We do know, however, that by the end of the first third of the nineteenth century, *nigger* had already become a familiar and influential insult.

In *A Treatise on the Intellectual Character and Civil and Political Condition of the Colored People of the United States: and the Preju-*

dice Exercised Towards Them (1837), Hosea Easton wrote that *nigger* "is an opprobrious term, employed to impose contempt upon [blacks] as an inferior race. . . . The term in itself would be perfectly harmless were it used only to distinguish one class of society from another; but it is not used with that intent. . . . [I]t flows from the fountain of purpose to injure." Easton averred that often the earliest instruction white adults gave to white children prominently featured the word *nigger*. Adults reprimanded them for being "worse than niggers," for being "ignorant as niggers," for having "no more credit than niggers"; they disciplined them by telling them that unless they behaved they would be carried off by "the old nigger" or made to sit with "niggers" or consigned to the "nigger seat," which was, of course, a place of shame.[5]

Nigger has seeped into practically every aspect of American culture, from literature to political debates, from cartoons to song. Throughout the 1800s and for much of the 1900s as well, writers of popular music generated countless lyrics that lampooned blacks, in songs such as "Philadelphia Riots; or, I Guess It Wasn't de Niggas Dis Time," "De Nigga Gal's Dream," "Who's Dat Nigga Dar A-Peepin?," "Run, Nigger, Run," "A Nigger's Reasons," "Nigger Will Be Nigger," "I Am Fighting for the Nigger," "Ten Little Niggers," "Niggas Git on de Boat," "Nigger in a Pit," "Nigger War Bride Blues," "Nigger, Nigger, Never Die," "Li'l Black Nigger," and "He's Just a Nigger." The chorus of this last begins, "He's just a nigger, when you've said dat you've said it all."[6]

Throughout American history, *nigger* has cropped up in children's rhymes, perhaps the best known of which is

5

Eeny-meeny-miney-mo!
Catch a nigger by the toe!
If he hollers, let him go!
Eeny-meeny-miney-mo!

But there are scores of others as well, including

Nigger, nigger, never die,
Black face and shiny eye.[7]

And then there is:

Teacher, teacher, don't whip me!
Whip that nigger behind that tree!
He stole honey and I stole money.
Teacher, teacher, wasn't that funny?[8]

Today, on the Internet, whole sites are devoted to nigger jokes. At KKKomedy Central–Micetrap's Nigger Joke Center, for instance, the "Nigger Ghetto Gazette" contains numerous jokes such as the following:

Q. What do you call a nigger boy riding a bike?
A. Thief!

Q. Why do niggers wear high-heeled shoes?
A. So their knuckles won't scrape the ground!

Q. What did God say when he made the first nigger?
A. "Oh, shit!"

Q. What do niggers and sperm have in common?
A. Only one in two million works!

Q. Why do decent white folk shop at nigger yard sales?
A. To get all their stuff back, of course!

Q. What's the difference between a pothole and a nigger?
A. You'd swerve to avoid a pothole, wouldn't you?

Q. How do you make a nigger nervous?
A. Take him to an auction.

Q. How do you get a nigger to commit suicide?
A. Toss a bucket of KFC into traffic.

Q. How do you keep niggers out of your backyard?
A. Hang one in the front yard.

Q. How do you stop five niggers from raping a white woman?
A. Throw them a basketball.[9]

Nigger has been a familiar part of the vocabularies of whites high and low. It has often been the calling card of so-called white trash—poor, disreputable, uneducated Euro-Americans. Partly to distance themselves from this ilk, some whites of higher standing have aggressively forsworn the use of *nigger*. Such was the case, for example, with senators Strom

Thurmond and Richard Russell, both white supremacists who never used the N-word. For many whites in positions of authority, however, referring to blacks as niggers was once a safe indulgence. Reacting to news that Booker T. Washington had dined at the White House, Senator Benjamin Tillman of South Carolina predicted, "The action of President Roosevelt in entertaining that nigger will necessitate our killing a thousand niggers in the South before they will learn their place again."[10] During his (ultimately successful) reelection campaign of 1912, the governor of South Carolina, Coleman Livingston Blease, declared with reference to his opponent, Ira Jones, the chief justice of the state supreme court, "You people who want social equality [with the Negro] vote for Jones. You men who have nigger children vote for Jones. You who have a nigger wife in your backyard vote for Jones."[11]

During an early debate in the United States House of Representatives over a proposed federal antilynching bill, black people sitting in the galleries cheered when a representative from Wisconsin rebuked a colleague from Mississippi for blaming lynching on Negro criminality. In response, according to James Weldon Johnson of the National Association for the Advancement of Colored People (NAACP), white southern politicians shouted from the floor of the House, "Sit down, niggers."[12] In 1938, when the majority leader of the United States Senate, Alben Barkley, placed antilynching legislation on the agenda, Senator James Byrnes of South Carolina (who would later become a supreme court justice and secretary of state) faulted the black NAACP official Walter White. Barkley,

Byrnes declared, "can't do anything without talking to that nigger first."[13]

Nigger was also a standard element in Senator Huey P. Long's vocabulary, though many blacks appreciated the Louisiana Democrat's notable reluctance to indulge in race baiting. Interviewing "The Kingfish" in 1935, Roy Wilkins (working as a journalist in the days before he became a leader of the NAACP) noted that Long used the terms "nigra," "colored," and "nigger" with no apparent awareness that that last word would or should be viewed as offensive.[14] By contrast, for Georgia governor Eugene Talmadge, *nigger* was not simply a designation he had been taught; it was also a tool of demagoguery that he self-consciously deployed. Asked by a white constituent about "Negroes attending our schools," Talmadge happily replied, "Before God, friend, the niggers will never go to a school which is white while I am governor."[15]

As in Georgia, so in Mississippi, where white judges routinely asked Negro defendants, "Whose nigger are you?"[16] Reporting a homicide, the Hattiesburg *Progress* noted: "Only another dead nigger—that's all."[17] Three decades later, the master of ceremonies at a White Citizens Council banquet would conclude the festivities by remarking, "Throughout the pages of history there is only one third-rate race which has been treated like a second-class race and complained about it—and that race is the American nigger."[18]

Nor was *nigger* confined to the language of local figures of limited influence. Supreme Court Justice James Clark McReynolds referred to Howard University as the "nigger university."[19] President Harry S Truman called Congressman Adam Clayton Powell "that damned nigger preacher."[20] *Nigger* was also in the vocabulary of Senator, Vice President, and President Lyndon Baines Johnson. "I talk everything over with [my wife]," he proclaimed on one occasion early in his political career. Continuing, he quipped, "Of course . . . I have a nigger maid, and I talk my problems over with her, too."[21]

A complete list of prominent whites who have referred at some point or other to blacks demeaningly as niggers would be lengthy indeed. It would include such otherwise disparate figures as Richard Nixon and Flannery O'Connor.[22]

Given whites' use of *nigger,* it should come as no surprise that for many blacks the N-word has constituted a major and menacing presence that has sometimes shifted the course of their lives. Former slaves featured it in their memoirs about bondage. Recalling her lecherous master's refusal to permit her to marry a free man of color, Harriet Jacobs related the following colloquy:

> "So you want to be married do you?" he said, "and to a free nigger."
> "Yes, sir."
> "Well, I'll soon convince you whether I am your master, or the nigger fellow you honor so highly. If you *must* have a husband, you may take up with one of my slaves."[23]

Nigger figures noticeably, too, in Frederick Douglass's autobiography. Re-creating the scene in which his master objected to his being taught to read and write, the great abolitionist imagined that the man might have said, "If you give a nigger an inch he will take an ell. A nigger should know nothing but to obey his master. . . . Learning would *spoil* the best nigger in the world."[24]

In the years since the Civil War, no one has more searingly dramatized *nigger*-as-insult than Richard Wright. Anyone who wants to learn in a brief compass what lies behind African American anger and anguish when *nigger* is deployed as a slur by whites should read Wright's *The Ethics of Living Jim Crow*. In this memoir about his life in the South during the teens and twenties of the twentieth century, Wright attacked the Jim Crow regime by showing its ugly manifestations in day-to-day racial interactions. Wright's first job took him to a small optical company in Jackson, Mississippi, where things went smoothly in the beginning. Then Wright made the mistake of asking the seventeen-year-old white youth with whom he worked to tell him more about the business. The youth viewed this sign of curiosity and ambition as an unpardonable affront. Wright narrated the confrontation that followed:

> "What yuh tryin' t' do, nigger, git smart?" he asked.
> "Naw; I ain' tryin' t' git smart," I said.
> "Well, don't, if yuh know what's good for yuh! . . . Nigger, you think you're *white,* don't you?"
> "No sir!"
> "This is *white* man's work around here, and you better watch yourself."[25]

From then on, the white youth so terrorized Wright that he ended up quitting.

At his next job, as a menial worker in a clothing store, Wright saw his boss and his son drag and kick a Negro woman into the store:

> Later the woman stumbled out, bleeding, crying, and holding her stomach. . . . When I went to the rear of the store, the boss and his son were washing their hands in the sink. They were chuckling. The floor was bloody and strewn with wisps of hair and clothing. No doubt I must have appeared pretty shocked, for the boss slapped me reassuringly on the back.
>
> "Boy, that's what we do to niggers when they don't want to pay their bills," he said, laughing.[26]

Along with intimidation, sex figured in Wright's tales of Negro life under segregationist tyranny. Describing his job as a "hall-boy" in a hotel frequented by prostitutes, the writer remembered

> a huge, snowy-skinned blonde [who] took a room on my floor. I was sent to wait upon her. She was in bed with a thick-set man; both were nude and uncovered. She said she wanted some liquor and slid out of bed and waddled across the floor to get her money from a dresser drawer. I watched her.
>
> "Nigger, what in hell you looking at?" the white man asked me, raising himself up on his elbows.

"Nothing," I answered, looking miles deep into the black wall of the room.

"Keep your eyes where they belong if you want to be healthy!" he said.

"Yes, sir."

On a different evening at this same hotel, Wright was leaving to walk one of the Negro maids home. As they passed by him, the white night watchman wordlessly slapped the maid on her buttock. Astonished, Wright instinctively turned around. His doing so, however, triggered yet another confrontation:

Suddenly [the night watchman] pulled his gun and asked: "Nigger, don't you like it?"

I hesitated.

"I asked yuh don't yuh like it?" he asked again, stepping forward.

"Yes, sir," I mumbled.

"Talk like it then!"

"Oh, yes, sir!" I said with as much heartiness as I could muster.

Outside, I walked ahead of the girl, ashamed to face her. She caught up with me and said: "Don't be a fool! Yuh couldn't help it!"

This watchman boasted of having killed two Negroes in self-defense.[27]

Among the ubiquitous stories featuring *nigger* that appear in literature by and about black Americans, several others also stand out.

In the summer of 1918, Lieutenant George S. Schuyler, proudly dressed in the uniform of the United States Army, stopped to get his boots shined at the Philadelphia railroad station. The bootblack, a recent immigrant from Greece, refused in a loud voice to serve "a nigger." This affront helped push Schuyler into going absent without leave, an infraction for which he was briefly imprisoned.[28] Although Schuyler became a writer and mined his own life for much of his material, this encounter with *nigger*-as-insult was so upsetting that he never publicly mentioned it.

In 1932 a young black Communist named Angelo Herndon found himself on trial for his life in Atlanta, Georgia, for allegedly organizing an insurrection. Testifying against him was a hostile witness who referred to him as a nigger. Herndon's black attorney, Benjamin Jefferson Davis, requested that the white judge intervene, prompting an ambiguous ruling:

> *Davis*: I object, Your Honor. The term "nigger" is objectionable, prejudicial, and insulting.
> *Judge Wyatt*: I don't know whether it is or not. . . . However, I'll instruct the witness to call [Herndon] "darky," which is a term of endearment.[29]

Radicalized by this experience, Davis himself soon thereafter joined the Communist party.

The civil rights activist Daisy Bates recalled an episode from her childhood in which a butcher refused to take her order until he had served all of the white customers in the shop, regardless of whether she had preceded them. "Niggers have to wait," the butcher stated.[30]

When a clerk at a drugstore soda fountain called him "nigger," nine-year-old Ely Green asked his foster mother what it meant. "Why should I be called a nigger?" he inquired. "It must be very bad to be a nigger." Bothered by her refusal or inability to explain, the boy spent a sleepless night trying to decipher the meaning of this mysterious word. "What could a nigger be," he wondered, and "why should God make me a nigger?"[31]

Paul Robeson earned a degree from Columbia Law School but turned his back on a career as an attorney after, among other incidents, a stenographer refused to work for him, declaring, "I never take dictation from a nigger."[32]

Malcolm X remembered that during his childhood, after his family fell apart following the murder of his father, the whites who served as his guardians openly referred to blacks as niggers. And then there was his encounter with a white teacher who, in recommending a career in carpentry rather than the law, urged young Malcolm to be "realistic about being a nigger."[33]

When Jackie Robinson reported to the Brooklyn Dodgers' top minor-league team, the manager earnestly asked the team's owner whether he really thought that niggers were human beings.[34] Robinson, of course, would have to contend with *nigger* throughout his fabled career. During a game played on April 22, 1947, he recalled hearing hatred pour forth from the dugout of the Philadelphia Phillies "as if it had been synchronized by some master conductor":

"Hey, nigger, why don't you go back to the cotton field where you belong?"

"They're waiting for you in the jungles, black boy!"

"We don't want you here, nigger."[35]

On a tour of the South in 1951, the journalist Carl Rowan tried to buy a newspaper in the white waiting room of a train depot since there were no papers in the colored waiting room. As he was about to pay, a white station agent hurriedly intervened to stop the transaction. Rowan complained that under the separate-but-equal theory of segregation he should be able to purchase any item in the colored waiting room that was available in the white waiting room. But the station agent was insistent:

"Well, you'll have to go back and let the redcap come and get the paper," he explained.

"The redcap? He's darker than I am and I've got the nickel—what's the logic there?" I argued.

"He's in uniform."

"Suppose I were in uniform—[the uniform] of the United States Navy?"

"You'd still have to go where niggers belong."[36]

In the early 1960s, at the height of his celebrity as a comedian, Dick Gregory ventured south to join other activists in protesting blacks' exclusion from the voting booth. In his autobiography, he recounted an altercation he had with a policeman in Greenwood, Mississippi, who, without just provocation, shoved him and ordered,

"Move on, nigger."

"Thanks a million."

"Thanks for what?"

"Up north police don't escort me across the street against the red light."

"I said, move on, nigger."

"I don't know my way, I'm new in this town."

The cop yanked on my arm and turned his head. "Send someone over to show this nigger where to go," he hollered. . . .

I pulled one of my arms free and pointed at the crowd.

"Ask that white woman over there to come here and show me where to go."

The cop's face got red, and there was spittle at the corner of his mouth. All he could say was: "Nigger, dirty nigger. . . ."

I looked at him. "Your momma's a nigger. Probably got more Negro blood in her than I could ever hope to have in me."

He dropped my other arm then, and backed away, and his hand was on his gun. I thought he was going to explode. But nothing happened. I was sopping wet and too excited to be scared.[37]

Either Gregory was lucky or his celebrity gave him more protection than others enjoyed. When Charles McLaurin, an organizer with the Student Nonviolent Coordinating Committee (SNCC), was jailed in Columbia, Mississippi, a patrolman asked him, "Are you a Negro or a nigger?" When

McLaurin responded, "Negro," another patrolman hit him in the face. When he gave the same reply to the same question, McLaurin was again beaten. Finally, asked the question a third time, he answered, "I am a nigger." At that point the first patrolman told him to leave town and warned, "If I ever catch you here again I'll kill you."[38]

As a child, the playwright August Wilson stopped going to school for a while after a series of notes were left in his desk by white classmates. The notes read: "Go home nigger."[39]

The Olympic sprinter Tommie Smith remembers an incident from his boyhood in which a white child snatched an ice cream cone out of his hand and snarled, "Niggers don't eat ice cream."[40]

Michael Jordan was suspended from school for hitting a white girl who called him "nigger" during a fight over a seat on a school bus in Wilmington, North Carolina.[41]

Tiger Woods was tied up in kindergarten by older schoolmates who called him "nigger."[42]

Recalling the difficulties she faced in raising her black son in a household with her white female lover, the poet Audre Lorde noted that "for years in the name-calling at school, boys shouted at [her son] not—'your mother's a lesbian'—but rather—'your mother's a nigger.' "[43]

The musician Branford Marsalis has said he cannot remember a time when he was *not* being called "nigger." "If you grew up in the South," he observed, whites "called you nigger from the time you were born."[44]

Reminiscing about the first time someone called her "nigger," the journalist Lonnae O'Neal Parker described a trip she took to Centralia, Illinois, with her parents when she was five years old. She was playing in a park when

> two white girls walked up to me. . . . They were big. Impossibly big. Eleven at least. They smiled at me.
>
> "Are you a nigger?" one of the girls asked. . . .
>
> I stood very still. And my stomach grew icy. . . . "I, I don't know," I told her, shrugging my shoulders high to my ears. . . .
>
> Then the other repeated, more forcefully this time, "Are you a nigger? You know, a black person?" she asked.
>
> I wanted to answer her. To say something. But fear made me confused. I had no words. I just stood there. And tried not to wet my panties.
>
> Then I ran.[45]

Responding to Parker's published recollection, a reader shared two stories of her own. Brenda Woodford wrote that in the predominantly white middle-class community where she grew up, little white boys on bicycles would constantly encircle her, chanting, "Nigger, nigger, nigger." Later Woodford continued to be shadowed by *nigger*. On one occasion, the word flew out of the mouth of a white man during an argument; at the time, she thought he loved her.[46]

In 1973, at the very moment he stood poised to break Babe Ruth's record for career home runs, the baseball superstar Hank Aaron encountered *nigger*-as-insult on a massive scale, largely in the form of hateful letters:

Dear Nigger,
Everybody loved Babe Ruth. You will be the most hated man in this country if you break his career home run record.

Dear Black Boy,
Listen Black Boy, we don't want no nigger Babe Ruth.

Dear Mr. Nigger,
I hope you don't break the Babe's record. How can I tell my kids that a nigger did it?

Dear Nigger,
You can hit all dem home runs over dem short fences, but you can't take dat black off yo face.

Dear Nigger,
You black animal, I hope you never live long enough to hit more home runs than the great Babe Ruth. . . .

Dear Nigger Henry,
You are [not] going to break this record established by the great Babe Ruth if you can help it. . . . Whites are far more superior than jungle bunnies. . . . My gun is watching your every black move.[47]

An offshoot of *nigger* is *nigger lover,* a label affixed to non-blacks who become friendly with African Americans or openly side with them in racial controversies. In the Civil War era,

Republicans' antislavery politics won them the appellation "black Republicans" or "nigger lovers." To discredit Abraham Lincoln, his racist Democratic party opponents wrote a "Black Republican Prayer" that ended with the "benediction"

> May the blessings of Emancipation extend throughout our unhappy land, and the illustrious, sweet-scented Sambo nestle in the bosom of every Abolition woman . . . and the distinction of color be forever consigned to oblivion [so] that we may live in bands of fraternal love, union and equality with the Almighty Nigger, henceforth, now and forever. Amen.[48]

One of Senator Charles Sumner's white constituents in Massachusetts suggested sneeringly that his exertions in favor of abolition amounted only to "riding the 'nigger' hobby."[49] Another dissatisfied constituent maintained that the senator suffered from "a deep-seated nigger cancer," that he could "speak of nothing but the 'sublime nigger,'" and that his speeches offered nothing but "the nigger at the beginning, nigger in the middle, and nigger at the end."[50]

A century later, during the civil rights revolution, whites who joined black civil rights protesters were frequently referred to as nigger lovers. When white and black "freedom riders" rode together on a bus in violation of (unlawful) local Jim Crow custom, a bigoted white driver took delight in delivering them to a furious crowd of racists in Anniston, Alabama. Cheerfully anticipating the beatings to come, the driver yelled to the mob, "Well, boys, here they are. I brought you some niggers and nigger lovers."[51] Speaking to a rally in Baltimore, Maryland, a spokesman for the National States Rights Party declared confidently that most "nigger lovers are sick in the mind" and "should be bound, hung, and killed."[52]

The term *nigger lover* continues to be heard amid the background noise that accompanies racial conflict. Whites who refrain from discriminating against blacks, whites who become intimate with blacks, whites who confront antiblack practices, whites who work on the electoral campaigns of black candidates, whites who nominate blacks for membership in clubs, whites who protect blacks in the course of their official duties, and whites who merely socialize with blacks are all subject to being derided as "nigger lovers."[53]

Over the years, *nigger* has become the best known of the American language's many racial insults, evolving into the paradigmatic slur. It is the epithet that generates epithets. That is why Arabs are called "sand niggers," Irish "the niggers of Europe," and Palestinians "the niggers of the Middle East"; why black bowling balls have been called "nigger eggs," games of craps "nigger golf," watermelons "nigger hams," rolls of one-dollar bills "nigger rolls," bad luck "nigger luck," gossip "nigger news," and heavy boots "nigger stompers."[54]

Observers have made strong claims on behalf of the special status of *nigger* as a racial insult. The journalist Farai Chideya describes it as "the all-American trump card, the nuclear bomb of racial epithets."[55] The writer Andrew Hacker has asserted that among slurs of any sort, *nigger* "stands alone [in] its power to tear at one's insides."[56] Judge Stephen Reinhardt deems *nigger* "the most noxious racial epithet in the contemporary American lexicon."[57] And prosecutor Christopher Darden famously branded *nigger* the "filthiest, dirtiest, nastiest word in the English language."[58]

The claim that *nigger* is the superlative racial epithet—the *most* hurtful, the *most* fearsome, the *most* dangerous, the *most* noxious—necessarily involves comparing oppressions and prioritizing victim status. Some scoff at this enterprise. Objecting to a columnist's assertion that being called a honky was not in the same league as being called a nigger, one reader responded, "We should be in the business of ending racism, not measuring on a politically correct thermometer the degree to which one is more victimized than another."[59] Declining to enter into a discussion comparing the Holocaust with American slavery, a distinguished historian quipped that he refused to become an accountant of atrocity. His demurral is understandable: sometimes the process of comparison degenerates into divisive competitions among minority groups that insist upon jealously defending their victim status.[60] Because the Jewish Holocaust is the best known and most widely vilified atrocity in modern times, many use it as an analogical yardstick for the purpose of highlighting their own tragedies. Hence Iris Chang dubbed the Japanese army's Rape of Nanking during World War II "the forgotten holocaust,"[61] Larry Kramer titled his reportage on the early days of the AIDS crisis *Reports from the Holocaust*,[62] and Toni Morrison dedicated her novel *Beloved* to the "sixty million and more"—a figure undoubtedly calculated to play off the familiar six million, the number of Jews generally thought to have perished at the hands of the Nazis.[63] At the same time, some who are intent upon propounding the uniqueness of the Holocaust aggressively reject analogies to it, as if comparing it to other atrocities could only belittle the Nazis' heinous crime.[64]

We could, of course, avoid making comparisons. Instead of saying that the Holocaust was the *worst* atrocity of the twentieth century, we could say simply that the Holocaust was terrible. Instead of saying that *nigger* has been the *most* socially destructive racial epithet in the American language, we could say merely that, when used derogatorily, *nigger* is a socially destructive epithet. Although such a strategy may have certain diplomatic merits, it deprives audiences of assistance in making qualitative judgments. After all, there is a difference between the massacre that kills fifty and the one that kills five hundred—or five thousand or fifty thousand. By the same token, the stigmatizing power of different racial insults can vary.

A comedy sketch dramatized by Richard Pryor and Chevy Chase on the television show *Saturday Night Live* makes this point vividly. Chase is interviewing Pryor for a job as a janitor and administers a word-association test that goes like this:

> " 'White,' " says Chase.
> " 'Black,' " Pryor replies.
> " 'Bean.' "
> " 'Pod.' "
> " 'Negro.' "
> " 'Whitey,' " Pryor replies lightly.
> " 'Tarbaby.' "

"What did you say?" Pryor asks, puzzled.

" 'Tarbaby,' " Chase repeats, monotone.

" 'Ofay,' " Pryor says sharply.

" 'Colored.' "

" 'Redneck!' "

" 'Jungle bunny!' "

" 'Peckerwood,' " Pryor yells.

" 'Burrhead!' "

" 'Cracker.' "

" 'Spearchucker!' "

" 'White trash!' "

" 'Jungle bunny!' "

" 'Honky!' "

" 'Spade!' "

" 'Honky, honky!' "

" 'Nigger,' " says Chase smugly [aware that, when pushed, he can always use that trump card].

" 'Dead honky!' " Pryor growls [resorting to the threat of violence now that he has been outgunned in the verbal game of racial insult].[65]

It is impossible to declare with confidence that when hurled as an insult, *nigger* necessarily inflicts more distress than other racial epithets. Individuals beset by thugs may well feel equally terrified whether those thugs are screaming "Kill the honky" or "Kill the nigger." In the aggregate, though, *nigger* is and has long been the most socially consequential racial insult. Consider, for example, the striking disparity of incidence that distinguishes *nigger* from other racial epithets appearing in reported court opinions. In reported federal and state cases in the LEXIS-NEXIS data base (as of July 2001), *kike* appears in eighty-four cases, *wetback* in fifty, *gook* in ninety, and *honky* in 286.[66] These cases reveal cruelty, terror, brutality, and heartache. Still, the frequency of these slurs is overwhelmed by that of *nigger,* which appears in 4,219 reported decisions.[67]

Reported court opinions are hardly a perfect mirror of social life in America; they are merely an opaque reflection that poses real difficulties of interpretation. The social meaning of litigation is ambiguous. It may represent an attempt to remedy real injury, or it may mark cynical exploitation of increased intolerance for racism. The very act of bringing a lawsuit may express a sense of empowerment, but declining to bring one may do so as well, signaling that a person or group has means other than cumbersome litigation by which to settle scores or vindicate rights. That there is more litigation in which *nigger* appears could mean that usage of the term is more prevalent than usage of analogous epithets; that its usage is associated with more dramatic injuries; that targets of *nigger* are more aggrieved or more willing and able to sue; or that authorities—police, prosecutors, judges, or juries—are more receptive to this species of complaint. I do not know which of these hypotheses best explains the salience of *nigger* in the jurisprudence of racial epithets. What cannot plausibly be doubted, however, is the fact of *nigger*'s baleful preeminence.

Nigger first appears in the reports of the United States Supreme Court in a decision announced in 1871. The case, *Blyew v. United States,*[68] dealt with the prosecution for murder of two white men who, for racial reasons, had hacked to death several members of a black family. According to a witness, one of the codefendants had declared that "there would soon be another war about the niggers" and that when it came, he "intended to go to killing niggers."[69]

In the years since, federal and state courts have heard hundreds of cases in which the word *nigger* figured in episodes of racially motivated violence, threats, and arson. Particularly memorable among these was the successful prosecution of Robert Montgomery for violation of federal criminal statutes.[70] In 1988, in Indianapolis, state authorities established a residential treatment center for convicted child molesters in an all-white neighborhood. From the center's opening until mid-1991—a period during which all of the residents of the center were white—neighbors voiced no objections. In June 1991, however, authorities converted the center into a shelter for approximately forty homeless veterans, twenty-five of whom were black. Soon thereafter trouble erupted as a group of whites, including Montgomery, loudly proclaimed their opposition to the encroachment of "niggers" and burned a cross and vandalized a car to express their feelings. An all-white cadre of child molesters was evidently acceptable, but the presence of blacks made a racially integrated group of homeless *veterans* intolerable!

If *nigger* represented only an insulting slur and was associated only with racial animus, this book would not exist, for the term would be insufficiently interesting to warrant extended study. *Nigger* is fascinating precisely because it has been put to a variety of uses and can radiate a wide array of meanings.

Unsurprisingly, blacks have often used *nigger* for different purposes than racist whites. To lampoon slavery, blacks created the story of the slave caught eating one of his master's pigs. "Yes, suh, Massa," the slave quipped, "you got less pig now, but you sho' got more nigger."[71] To poke fun at the grisly phenomenon of lynching, African Americans told of the black man who, upon seeing a white woman pass by, said, "Lawd, will I ever?" A white man responded, "No, nigger, never." The black man replied, "Where there's life, there's hope." And the white man declared, "Where there's a nigger, there's a rope."[72] To dramatize the tragic reality of Jim Crow subjugation, African Americans recounted the tale of the Negro who got off a bus down south. Seeing a white policeman, he politely asked for the time. The policeman hit him twice with a club and said, "Two o'clock, nigger. Why?" "No reason, Cap'n," the black man answered. "I's just glad it ain't twelve."[73] And to satirize "legal" disenfranchisement, African Americans told the joke about the black man who attempted to register to vote. After the man answered a battery of questions that were far more difficult than any posed to whites, an official confronted him with a headline in a Chinese paper and demanded a translation. "Yeah, I know what it means," the black man said. "It means that niggers don't vote in Mississippi again this year."[74]

In the 1960s and 1970s, protest became more direct and more assertive. Drafted to fight a "white man's war" in Vietnam, Muhammad Ali refused to be inducted into the U.S. Army, explaining, "No Vietcong ever called me 'nigger.' "[75] Emphasizing the depth of white racism all across the United

States, activists joked, "What is a Negro with a Ph.D.?" Their response? "Dr. Nigger."

In his famous "Letter from a Birmingham Jail," Martin Luther King Jr. continued to agitate, listing in wrenching detail the indignities that prompted his impatience with tardy reform. He cited having to sleep in automobiles because of racial exclusion from motels, having to explain to his children why they could not go to amusement parks open to the white public, and being "harried by day and haunted by night by the fact that you are a Negro, living constantly at tip-toe stance never quite knowing what to expect next." Among King's litany of abuses was the humiliating way in which whites routinely addressed blacks: "Your wife and mother," he observed, "are never given the respected title 'Mrs.,' " and under the etiquette of Jim Crow, "your first name becomes 'nigger' and your middle name becomes 'boy' (however old you are) and your last name becomes 'John.' "[76]

For some observers, the only legitimate use of *nigger* is as a rhetorical boomerang against racists. There are others, however, who approvingly note a wide range of additional usages. According to Professor Clarence Major, when *nigger* is "used by black people among themselves, [it] is a racial term with undertones of warmth and good will—reflecting . . . a tragicomic sensibility that is aware of black history."[77] The writer Claude Brown once admiringly described *nigger* as "perhaps the most soulful word in the world,"[78] and journalist Jarvis DeBerry calls it "beautiful in its multiplicity of functions." "I am not aware," DeBerry writes, "of any other word capable of expressing so many contradictory emotions."[79] Traditionally an insult, *nigger* can also be a compliment, as in "He played like a nigger." Historically a signal of hostility, it can also be a salutation announcing affection, as in "This is my main nigger." A term of belittlement, *nigger* can also be a term of respect, as in "James Brown is a straight-up nigger." A word that can bring forth bitter tears in certain circumstances, *nigger* can prompt joyful laughter in others.[80]

A candid portrayal of the N-word's use among African Americans may be found in Helen Jackson Lee's autobiography, *Nigger in the Window*. It was Lee's cousin who first introduced her to *nigger*'s possibilities. As Lee remembered it, "Cousin Bea had a hundred different ways of saying *nigger*; listening to her, I learned the variety of meanings the word could assume. How it could be opened like an umbrella to cover a dozen different moods, or stretched like a rubber band to wrap up our family with other colored families. . . . *Nigger* was a piece-of-clay word that you could shape . . . to express your feelings."[81]

Nigger has long been featured in black folk humor. There is the story, for example, of the young boy inspired by a minister's sermon on loving all of God's creatures. Finding a frozen rattlesnake, he nicely put the animal under his shirt to warm it up. "Nigger, I'm gonna bite the hell out of you!" the snake announced upon its revival. "Mr. Snake," the boy asked, "you mean to say you gonna bite me after I followed the preacher's teaching and took you to my bosom?" "Hell yeah, nigger," the snake replied. "You knew I was a snake, didn't you?"[82]

Before the 1970s, however, *nigger* seldom figured in the

routines of professional comedians. It was especially rare in the acts of those who performed for racially mixed audiences. Asserting that unmentionable slurs derived much of their seductive power from their taboo status, the iconoclastic white comedian Lenny Bruce recommended a strategy of subversion through overuse. In a 1963 routine, Bruce suggested with characteristic verve that "if President Kennedy got on television and said, 'Tonight I'd like to introduce the niggers in my cabinet,' and he yelled 'Niggerniggerniggerniggerniggerniggernigger' at every nigger he saw . . . till *nigger* didn't mean anything anymore, till *nigger* lost its meaning . . . you'd never hear any four-year-old nigger cry when he came home from school."[83]

But Bruce was unusual, and in terms of the N-word, he failed to inspire emulation. While the hip comedians of the 1950s and 1960s—Dick Gregory, Nipsey Russell, Mort Sahl, Godfrey Cambridge, Moms Mabley, Redd Foxx—told sexually risqué or politically barbed jokes, *nigger* for the most part remained off-limits.

All that changed with the emergence of Richard Pryor.[84] Through live performances and a string of albums, he brought *nigger* to center stage in stand-up comedy, displaying with consummate artistry its multiple meanings.

Pryor's single best performance may be heard on the aptly titled *That Nigger's Crazy,* winner of the 1974 Grammy Award for best comedy recording. The album explores Pryor's professional fears ("Hope I'm funny . . . because I know niggers ready to kick ass"), blacks' alleged ability to avoid certain sorts of danger ("Niggers never get burned up in buildings. . . .

White folks just panic, run to the door, fall all over each other. . . . Niggers get outside, *then* argue"), black parenting styles ("My father was one of them eleven-o'clock niggers"), comparative sociology ("White folks fuck quiet; niggers make noise"), racial anthropology ("White folks . . . don't know how to play the dozens"), and social commentary ("Nothin' can scare a nigger after four hundred years of this shit").

The bit that often provokes the most applause from black listeners is Pryor's "Niggers vs. Police":

> Cops put a hurtin' on your ass, man, y'know? They really degrade you.
>
> White folks don't believe that shit, don't believe cops degrade you. [They say,] "Oh, c'mon, those people were resisting arrest. I'm tired of this harassment of police officers." Police live in [a white] neighborhood, and [all his white neighbors] be knowin' the man as Officer Timson. "Hello, Officer Timson, going bowling tonight? Yes, nice Pinto you have. Ha, ha."
>
> Niggers don't know 'em like that. See, white folks get a ticket, they pull over [and say], "Hey Officer, yes, glad to be of help." Nigger got to be talkin' about "I am reaching into my pocket for my license! 'Cause I don't wanta be no muthafuckin' accident!"

Mel Watkins has rightly maintained that what made Richard Pryor a pathbreaking figure was that he "introduce[d] and popularize[d] that unique, previously concealed or rejected part of

African-American humor that thrived in the lowest, most unassimilated portion of the black community."[85] He broke free, at least for a while, of all those—whites and blacks alike—who, sometimes for different reasons, shared an aversion to too much realism. He seemed radically unconcerned with deferring to any social conventions, particularly those that accepted black comedians as clowns but rejected them as satirists. Nothing more vividly symbolized his defiant, risk-taking spirit than his unprecedented playfulness regarding the explosive N-word in performances before racially mixed audiences.[86]

In the years since the release of *That Nigger's Crazy,* the N-word has become a staple in the routine of many black comedians. Among these, the one who most jarringly deploys it is Chris Rock, whose signature skit begins with the declaration "I love black people, but I hate niggers." He goes on:

> It's like our own personal civil war.
> On the one side, there's black people.
> On the other, you've got niggers.
> The niggers have got to go. Every time black people want to have a good time, niggers mess it up. You can't do anything without some ignorant-ass niggers fucking it up.
> Can't go to a movie the first week it opens. Why? Because niggers are shooting at the screen. . . .
> You can't have anything in your house. Why? Because the niggers who live next door will break in, take it all,

and then come over the next day and go, "We heard you got robbed."

According to Rock, "niggers always want credit for some shit they're *supposed* to do. They'll say something like 'I took care of my kids.' "Exploding with impatience, Rock interjects:

You're *supposed* to, you dumb motherfucker.
"I ain't never been to jail."
Whaddya want? A cookie? You're not *supposed* to go to jail, you low-expectation-having motherfucker.

Rock asserts that "the worst thing about niggers is that they love to *not know*." That's because, he says, "niggers don't read. Books are like Kryptonite to a nigger."

Aware that some may condemn his routine as latter-day minstrelsy, racial betrayal, or a false pandering to antiblack prejudice, Rock exclaims near the end of his performance,

I know what all you black [listeners] think.
"Man, why you got to say that? . . . It isn't us, it's the *media*. The media has distorted our image to make us look bad. Why must you come down on us like that, brother? It's not us, it's the media."
Please cut the shit. When I go to the money machine at night, I'm not looking over my shoulder for the media.
I'm looking for niggers.
Ted Koppel never took anything from me. Niggers have. Do you think I've got three guns in my house because the media's outside my door trying to bust in?[87]

Rap is another genre of entertainment suffused with instances of *nigger*. A cursory survey just of titles yields Dr. Dre's "The Day the Niggas Took Over," A Tribe Called Quest's "Sucka Nigga," Jaz-Z's "Real Nigger," the Geto Boys' "Trigga Happy Nigga," DMX's "My Niggas," and Cypress Hill's "Killa Hill Nigga." In "Gangsta's Paradise," meanwhile, Coolio declares,

> *I'm the kind of nigga*
> *little homies want to be like*
> *on their knees in the night*
> *saying prayers in the streetlights.*[88]

Ice-T says in one of his songs, "I'm a nigger not a colored man or a black or a Negro or an Afro-American."[89] Ice Cube, for his part, dubs himself "the Nigga ya love to hate,"[90] And Beanie Sigel promises

> *I'ma ride with my niggas*
> *die with my niggas*
> *get high with my niggas*
> *split pies with my niggas*
> *till my body gets hard*
> *soul touch the sky*
> *till my numbers get called*
> *and God shuts my eyes.*[91]

One of the seminal influences in gangsta rap called itself N.W.A, short for "Niggaz Wit Attitude." One of this group's most popular albums was *Efil4zaggin,* which, read backward, is "Niggaz 4 Life." Tupac Shakur proclaimed that for him, *nigga* stood for "Never Ignorant, Gets Goals Accomplished."[92]

Some people—I call them eradicationists—seek to drive *nigger* out of rap, comedy, and all other categories of entertainment even when (perhaps *especially* when) blacks themselves are the ones using the N-word. They see this usage as bestowing legitimacy on *nigger* and misleading those whites who have little direct interaction with African Americans. Eradicationists also maintain that blacks' use of *nigger* is symptomatic of racial self-hatred or the internalization of white racism, thus the rhetorical equivalent of black-on-black crime.

There is something to both of these points. The use of *nigger* by black rappers and comedians has given the term a new currency and enhanced cachet such that many young whites yearn to use the term like the blacks whom they see as heroes or trendsetters. It is undoubtedly true, moreover, that in some cases, blacks' use of *nigger* is indicative of an antiblack, self-hating prejudice. I myself first became aware of the term as a child in an all-black setting—my family household in Columbia, South Carolina—in which older relatives routinely attributed to negritude traits they disparaged, including tardiness, dishonesty, rudeness, impoverishment, cowardice, and stupidity. Such racial disparagement *of* blacks *by* blacks was by no means idiosyncratic. It is a widespread feature of African American culture that has given rise to a distinctive corpus of racial abasement typified by admonishments, epigraphs, and doggerel such as:

Stop acting like a nigger.

I don't want nothing black but a Cadillac.[93]

Niggers and flies. Niggers and flies. The more I see niggers, the more I like flies.[94]

If you're white, you're right,
If you're yellow, you're mellow,
If you're brown, stick around,
If you're black, step back.[95]

This tendency toward racial self-abnegation has been much diminished since the civil rights revolution. But it still retains a grip on the psyches of many black Americans and is searingly evident in a phrase well known in black circles: "Niggers ain't shit."[96]

Self-hatred, however, is an implausible explanation for why many assertive, politically progressive African Americans continue to say "nigger" openly and frequently in conversations with one another. These are African Americans who, in their own minds at least, use *nigger* not in subjection to racial subordination but in defiance of it. Some deploy a long tradition, especially evident in black nationalist rhetoric, of using abusive criticism to spur action that is intended to erase any factual predicate for the condemnation voiced. An example is writing by the Last Poets, a group established in 1968 that merged poetry, music, and politics in forms that anticipated certain types of rap. A famous item in the Last Poets' repertoire was "Niggers Are Scared of Revolution," in which they charged that:

> Niggers are scared of revolution but niggers shouldn't be scared of revolution because revolution is nothing but change, and all niggers do is change. Niggers come in from work and change into pimping clothes to hit the streets to make some quick change. Niggers change their hair from black to red to blond and hope like hell their looks will change. Niggers kill other niggers just because one didn't receive the correct change. . . .
>
> Niggers shoot dope into their arms. Niggers shoot guns and rifles on New Year's Eve, a new year that is coming in where white police will do more shooting at them. Where are niggers when the revolution needs some shot? Yeah . . . you know, niggers are somewhere shooting the shit. Niggers are scared of revolution.[97]

Describing their intentions, Umar Bin Hassan writes that the poem constituted a "call to arms" because "niggers are human beings lost in somebody else's system of values and morals."[98]

Many blacks also do with *nigger* what other members of marginalized groups have done with slurs aimed at shaming them. They have thrown the slur right back in their oppressors' faces. They have added a positive meaning to *nigger*, just as women, gays, lesbians, poor whites, and children born out of wedlock have defiantly appropriated and revalued such words as *bitch, cunt, queer, dyke, redneck, cracker*, and *bastard*.[99]

Yet another source of allegiance to *nigger* is a pessimistic view of the African American predicament. Many blacks who use *nigger* in public before racially mixed audiences disdain dressing up their colloquial language. They do not even attempt to put their best foot forward for the purpose of impressing whites or eroding stereotypes because they see such missions as lost causes. They like to use *nigger* because it is a shorthand way of reminding themselves and everyone else precisely where they perceive themselves as standing in American society—the message being, "Always remember you's a nigger." As Bruce A. Jacobs observes, "To proclaim oneself a nigger is to declare to the disapproving mainstream, 'You can't fire me. I quit.' Hence the perennial popularity of the word. Among poor black youth who . . . carry a burning resentment of white society. To growl that one is a nigga is a seductive gesture . . . that can feel bitterly empowering."[100]

Two additional considerations also warrant notice here, both of them having to do with the power of words to simultaneously create and divide communities. Some blacks use *nigger* to set themselves off from Negroes who refuse to use it. To proclaim oneself a nigger is to identify oneself as real, authentic, uncut, unassimilated, and unassimilable—the opposite, in short, of a Negro, someone whose rejection of *nigger* is seen as part of an effort to blend into the white mainstream. Sprinkling one's language with *nigger*s is thus a way to "keep it real."[101]

Roping off cultural turf is another aim of some blacks who continue to use *nigger* in spite of its stigmatized status. Certain forms of black cultural expression have become commercially valuable, and black cultural entrepreneurs fear that these forms will be exploited by white performers who will adopt them and, tapping white-skin privilege, obtain compensation far outstripping that paid to black performers. This is, of course, a realistic fear in light of the long history of white entertainers' becoming rich and famous by marketing in whiteface cultural innovations authored by their underappreciated black counterparts. A counterstrategy is to seed black cultural expression with gestures that are widely viewed as being off-limits to whites. Saying "nigger" is one such gesture. Even whites who immerse themselves in black hip-hop culture typically refrain from openly and unabashedly saying "nigger" like their black heroes or colleagues, for fear that it might be perceived as a sign of disrespect rather than one of solidarity.

Some nonwhite entertainers have used *nigger* in their acts. John Lennon and Yoko Ono, for example, entitled a song "Woman Is the Nigger of the World,"[102] and Patti Smith wrote "Rock 'n' Roll Nigger."[103] But Lennon, Ono, and Smith performed in overwhelmingly white milieus. Rap, by contrast, is dominated by blacks. A few white rappers have achieved commercial success and won the respect of black artists and audiences. I am thinking here especially of the white rapper Eminem, a superstar in the hip-hop culture. Eminem has assumed many of the distinctive mannerisms of his black rap colleagues, making himself into a "brother" in many ways—in his music, his diction, his gait, his clothes, his associations. He refuses to say, however, any version of a word that his black hip-hop colleagues employ constantly as a matter of course; the nonchalance with which he tosses around epithets such as *bitch* and *faggot* does not extend to *nigger*. "That word," he insists, "is not even in my vocabulary."[104]

Eminem is certainly following a prudent course, for many people, white and black alike, disapprove of a white person saying "nigger" under virtually any circumstance. "When we call each other 'nigger' it means no harm," Ice Cube remarks. "But if a white person uses it, it's something different, it's a racist word."[105] Professor Michael Eric Dyson likewise asserts that whites must know and stay in their racial place when it comes to saying "nigger." He writes that "most white folk attracted to black culture know better than to cross a line drawn in the sand of racial history. *Nigger* has never been cool when spit from white lips."[106]

The race line that Dyson applauds, however, is a specious divide. There is nothing necessarily wrong with a white person saying "nigger," just as there is nothing necessarily wrong with a black person saying it. What should matter is the context in which the word is spoken—the speaker's aims, effects, alternatives. To condemn whites who use the N-word without regard to context is simply to make a fetish of *nigger*. Harriet Beecher Stowe (*Uncle Tom's Cabin*), Mark Twain (*Huckleberry Finn*), William Dean Howells (*An Imperative Duty*), Edward Sheldon (*The Nigger*), Eugene O'Neill (*All God's Chillun*), Lillian Smith (*Strange Fruit*), Sinclair Lewis (*Kingsblood Royal*), Joyce Carol Oates (*Them*), E. L. Doctorow (*Ragtime*), John Grisham (*A Time to Kill*), and numerous other white writers have unveiled *nigger*-as-insult in order to dramatize and condemn racism's baleful presence.

In 1967, President Lyndon Baines Johnson decided to

appoint an African American to the Supreme Court for the first time in American history. First on Johnson's list of candidates was Thurgood Marshall—"Mr. Civil Rights," the hero of *Brown v. Board of Education* and, of course, the man he ended up putting on the Court. But before he announced his selection, Johnson asked an assistant to identify some other possible candidates. The aide mentioned A. Leon Higginbotham, whom Johnson had appointed to the federal trial bench. Reportedly, the president dismissed the suggestion with the comment "The only two people who have ever heard of Judge Higginbotham are you and his momma. When I appoint a nigger to the [Supreme Court], I want everyone to know he's a nigger."[107] Was the use of *nigger* in this context a venting of racial prejudice? Maybe. Johnson had been raised in a thoroughly racist environment, had supported racist policies for a long period, and, as we have seen, casually used *nigger* as part of his private vocabulary before he became president. On this particular occasion, however, it seems likely that he was merely seeking to highlight the racial exclusion against which he was acting, parodying the old regime even as he sought to reform it. If this is an accurate assessment of the situation, I see nothing wrong with what Johnson said, and I applaud what he did.

Can a relationship between a black person and a white one be such that the white person should properly feel authorized, at least within the confines of that relationship, to use the N-word? For me the answer is yes. Carl Van Vechten, for instance, wrote of "niggers" in correspondence with his friend Langston Hughes,[108] and Hughes did not object (though he did once write that *nigger* was a red flag for all Negroes).[109] *Should*

Hughes have objected? No. Van Vechten, a key supporter of the Harlem Renaissance, had shown time and again that he abhorred racial prejudice, would do what he could to improve the fortunes of African Americans, and treasured his black friends. It was against this backdrop of achieved trust that Hughes (and other black writers) rightly permitted Van Vechten to use *nigger* as so many African Americans have used it—as an ironic, shorthand spoof on the absurdity of American race relations.[110]

As we have seen, *nigger* can mean many different things, depending upon, among other variables, intonation, the location of the interaction, and the relationship between the speaker and those to whom he is speaking. Generally a reference to people of color, particularly blacks, *nigger* can refer to people of any hue. Senator Robert C. Byrd (D–West Virginia) got into trouble for saying publicly that he "had seen a lot of white niggers in [his] time."[111] But more and more the word is being applied ecumenically. Sociologist John Hartigan reports that poor whites in Detroit often refer to their white neighbors as *niggers*.[112] Typically they mean the word as an insult. But they do not necessarily mean for it to be a *racial* insult. Responding to an inquiry about a white-on-white deployment of *nigger*, one of the participants in Hartigan's study remarked: "He's a nigger, man, and you know what I mean by that. He's an asshole, and it doesn't matter whether a person's black or white, orange or plaid, he can still be a nigger if he runs his mouth like that asshole."[113] Another white Detroiter observed by Hartigan echoed this sentiment. "You don't have to be black to be a nigger," he declared. "Niggers come in all colors."

(Interestingly, he added: "We are all colored. . . . There's about a hundred shades of white.")[114]

The linguist Arthur K. Spears has also discerned an appreciable revision of *nigger*'s racial usage. He writes that "White public school teachers hear themselves referred to as 'that White nigga' or simply 'nigga,' and [that] Asian Americans in San Francisco can be heard, as they navigate high school hallways, to call one another niggas."[115]

More vividly than most words, then, *nigger* illustrates Justice Oliver Wendell Holmes's observation that "a word is not a crystal, transparent and unchanged." A word is instead "the skin of a living thought [that] may vary greatly in color and content according to the circumstances and the time in which it is used."[116]

CHAPTER TWO

Nigger in Court

In September 1957, Congressman Charles C. Diggs Jr. of Michigan traveled to Sumner, Mississippi, to see firsthand the trial of two white men charged with the murder of a black fourteen-year-old from Chicago. Emmett Till had been killed for violating Jim Crow etiquette by, among other things, whistling at the wife of one of the defendants. In Sumner, Diggs encountered segregation in full bloom. Greeting a bevy of black reporters from across the country, the local sheriff cheerfully shouted, "Hello, niggers," without a hint of self-consciousness. One of these reporters, James Hicks of the *Amsterdam News,* sought to secure a seat in the segregated courtroom for Representative Diggs. Professor Stephen J. Whitfield tells what happened:

> Diggs had wired Judge Curtis L. Swango of the Seventeenth Judicial District to ask whether he might attend

the trial. The judge, a tall, informal forty-seven-year-old, a graduate of Millsaps College in Jackson and of the law school at "Ole Miss," invited him down. But by the time the representative got inside the courtroom, the whites and then the blacks had already taken all the seats. Diggs gave his card to Hicks, who started to walk up to the judge's bench but was accosted by a deputy who inquired: "Where you going, nigger?" When Hicks explained his mission and showed the deputy the card, another deputy was called over and told: "This nigger said there's a nigger outside who says he's a Congress-man. . . ."

"A nigger Congressman?"

"That's what this nigger said," and then the first deputy laughed at so blatant a contradiction in terms. But the sheriff was summoned and then told Hicks: "I'll bring him in here, but I'm going to sit him at you niggers' table." And that is where the representative sat.[1]

Although *nigger* was in the air throughout the Emmett Till case—from the promising indictment to the appalling acquittal—debate over the word did not play a central role in the litigation. In many other cases, though, such debate has occupied a salient place in the legal wrangling, generating a distinctive jurisprudence that can be divided into at least four categories. The first of these comprises cases in which a party seeks relief after it is revealed that officials within the criminal justice system—jurors, lawyers, or judges—have referred to blacks as niggers. The second encompasses cases in which an individual who kills another seeks to have his culpability diminished on the grounds that he was provoked when the other party called him a nigger. The third type of case involves controversies surrounding targets of racial invective who sue for damages under tort law or antidiscrimination statutes. And the fourth category consists of situations in which a judge must decide whether or not to permit jurors to be told about the linguistic habits of witnesses or litigants.

In 1978 in Columbus, Georgia, a jury handed down a death sentence for one William Henry Hance, who had committed multiple murders. After the trial two jurors revealed that they had heard fellow jurors make racially derogatory remarks about the defendant. More specifically, one juror maintained that during their deliberation, other jurors had referred to Hance as a "typical nigger" and "just one more sorry nigger that no one would miss." No court investigated the accuracy of these allegations prior to Hance's execution.[2]

Any defendant who seeks to challenge a conviction or sentence on the basis of prejudiced jury deliberations is very unlikely to prevail. First, federal and state rules of evidence stringently exclude juror testimony that impeaches a jury's verdict. And second, many jurisdictions require defendants to show actual prejudice resulting from juror misconduct.[3]

It is understandable that the legal system should want to promote finality, protect jurors from harassment, and shield the privacy and independence of jury deliberations. Still, it is chilling to think that a person could be sentenced to death pursuant to deliberations tainted by *nigger*.[4] The use of the word raises concerns not only about the attitudes of the jurors who said it but also about the attitudes of the jurors who *heard* it. In 1985 social psychologists Jeff Greenberg and Tom Pyszczynki performed an experiment aimed at determining how listeners were affected by overhearing racial slurs directed at specific targets. They asked groups of white college students to judge debates between white and black contestants. Immediately after the debates, persons working in concert with the experimenters either derogatorily referred to the black contestants as niggers, criticized them in a nonracist manner, or made no comment at all. Greenberg and Pyszczynki found that observers who overheard the insult exhibited a marked tendency to lower their evaluation of the slurred black debaters. This suggested, the researchers argued, that racial slurs "can indeed cue prejudiced behavior in those who are exposed to [such slurs]," a phenomenon that could well have practical significance in such settings as "parole board meetings, promotion committee meetings, and jury deliberations, in which [racial] slurs may be expressed by one member of a group, be overheard, and then affect the evaluations of the target by other members of the group." *Nigger,* Greenberg and Pyszczynki concluded, was not merely a symptom of prejudice but a carrier of the disease.[5] The risk in *Hance* was thus not simply that the manifest racial prejudice of two jurors might have eroded *their* ability to determine facts and set an appropriate punishment, but also that the use of *nigger* might have transmitted the pair's prejudice to other jurors, awakening latent biases or creating racial animus where none had previously existed.

Judges, too, use the N-word. In the late 1960s, H. Rap Brown, the former head of the Student Nonviolent Coordinating Committee (SNCC), was convicted of a firearms violation. After the conviction, a lawyer stepped forward with information suggesting that the judge who had presided over the trial harbored a prejudice against Brown. According to this lawyer, the judge had said that he was "going to get that nigger."[6] At a postconviction hearing, a new judge found the lawyer's statement to be credible but decided nonetheless to affirm the conviction and sentence. He ruled that notwithstanding the initial judge's unfortunate comment, the defendant had had a fair trial. The court of appeals subsequently reversed his decision and vacated Brown's conviction. In doing so, it relied on a federal statute that requires the mandatory disqualification of a judge " 'in any proceeding in which his impartiality might reasonably be questioned' or 'where he has a personal bias or prejudice concerning a party.' "[7] The court of appeals emphasized that the trial judge's remark had undercut the appearance of impartiality. It also concluded that it could not suitably determine from the trial record alone whether or not the defendant had received a fair trial.

The reversal of Brown's conviction is an inspiration compared to *Hance*. Still, there remains the disquiet of knowing that the judge remained in office, in a position to adjudicate disputes involving others whom he may well have called niggers in private. How must it have felt to be a black litigant in Judge Lansing L. Mitchell's courtroom the day *after* the reversal of H. Rap Brown's conviction?

This raises the question of what should be done about officials such as Judge Mitchell. The federal Constitution offers great—in my view *excessive*—security to federal judges inasmuch as they cannot be removed from office except by the famously cumbersome process of impeachment by the United States House of Representatives and conviction by the United States Senate. Other jurisdictions are able to handle matters of judicial bias more expediently. In 1994, for example, the California Supreme Court suspended Judge Stanley Z. Goodfarb for making repeated derogatory references to "niggers" off the record in his chambers, where he believed himself to be immune from the disapproval of observers.[8] In 1998 the Supreme Court of Michigan removed a judge who, in tapes surreptitiously made by her husband, was revealed as a person who constantly referred to blacks demeaningly as niggers.[9]

In 1999 a state court in New York removed J. Kevin Mulroy from a judgeship based on several incidents. In one case, Judge Mulroy had attempted to persuade a prosecutor to accept a plea bargain from four men indicted for murdering and robbing a sixty-seven-year-old African American woman. The judge told the prosecutor that he should not worry about the case since the victim had been just "some old nigger bitch."[10] In castigating Mulroy for this remark, the court observed that he had "devalued the life of the victim in a most non-professional, disturbing, and inappropriate way. . . . A judge's use of such language indicates an unacceptable bias and insensitivity that [have] no place on the bench and [warrant] the severest possible sanction."[11]

Case law documents instances in which prosecutors in open court have referred to African American defendants as niggers.[12] In 1911 a Mississippi prosecutor told a jury, "This bad nigger killed a good nigger. The dead nigger was a white man's nigger and these bad niggers like to kill that kind. The only way you can break up this pistol toting among these niggers is to have a necktie party."[13] (Decades later, the good nigger/bad nigger distinction would remain in force: explaining why he had killed a black man and his wife shortly after World War II, one white bigot recalled, "Up until George went into the Army, he was a good Nigger. But when he came out, [he and his wife] thought they were as good as any white people.")[14] In 1907 a prosecutor in Texas stated that he was well enough acquainted with a certain "class of niggers to know that they have got it in for the [white] race."[15] A prosecutor in Alabama in 1922 demanded of a presumably all-white jury, "Are you gentlemen going to believe that nigger [defendant] sitting over there . . . in preference to the testimony of [white] deputies?"[16] A prosecutor in Texas in 1970 asked a witness if he would have gotten out of his car "for three nigger men at night if they hadn't had guns."[17] Although there has long been a consensus that such slurs are prohibited, courts have generally declined to reverse convictions stemming from proceedings in which the N-word was used if the trial judge admonished the prosecutor and instructed the jury to disregard the offending language. Such was the outcome, for example, in the 1922 and 1970 cases described above. Appellate judges are understandably loath to award a windfall to a vicious criminal who happens to have been prosecuted by an undisciplined bigot. That is why they tend to uphold convictions provided they have some indication that the original trials were not irredeemably polluted by racist language. There is no good excuse, though, for the general failure of judges and local bar associations to discipline lawyers who demean courtroom proceedings with blatantly racist language. I have never heard of a case in which a prosecutor faced discipline for using an insulting version of *nigger* in the courtroom.

In one remarkable case, however, a prosecutor was disciplined for using the N-word outside of court.[18] In the early-morning hours of June 30, 1995, Jerry L. Spivey, the elected district attorney of the Fifth Prosecutorial District of North Carolina, got inebriated in a bar in Wrightsville Beach and was heard to say regarding another patron, "Look at that nigger hitting on my wife." The patron to whom he was referring was Ray Jacobs, a professional football player with the Denver Broncos who had previously been a college star in North Carolina. A little later, when Spivey's wife sought to introduce the two men and began by asking her husband whether he recognized Jacobs, the district attorney responded by saying, "He looks like a nigger to me." That comment was followed by others in which District Attorney Spivey, with an increasing degree of drunken agitation, repeatedly referred to Jacobs as a nigger. Eventually the bartender ejected the district attorney from the establishment.[19]

Soon thereafter, several attorneys petitioned a judge to remove Spivey from his post pursuant to a state law authorizing such an action in the event of misconduct prejudicial to the administration of justice and bringing an office into disrepute. During a hearing, expert testimony was elicited from the distinguished historian John Hope Franklin on the history and meaning of the word *nigger*. The judge also heard testimony from other members of the community who told the court about experiences they had had with the N-word and described their perception of the district attorney in light of his racial language. One man recounted the following painful memory from his days in the Air Force in the 1950s: "I was coming in from an overseas assignment and I stopped in Arkansas to get some gas and a sandwich. Three kids with me. We walked up, put the gas in the car. Stopped at the side window to get a sandwich and from the inside we were told, 'We don't serve niggers here.' I said, 'We simply want to get a sandwich.' He took my money for the gas and we turned and walked [away]. My little kid asked me, 'Daddy, what's a nigger?' "[20] Questioned about the effect that incident had had on him, the man responded tearfully that he had never stopped hurting. When asked to react to the district attorney's use of the N-word, he remarked, "To me it says that it doesn't matter what you have accomplished in life . . . if you have a black face . . . you are less than a person."[21]

The judge removed Spivey from office. The former district attorney appealed, arguing, among other things, that his federal First Amendment rights had been violated. There was some irony in his claiming that the state had wrongfully punished him for giving voice to protected expression, since he simultaneously insisted that what he had said did not at all express his true sentiments or beliefs. "I am sorry," he testified, that "I used the word *nigger*. . . . That word occupies no place in my day-to-day vocabulary, and that word in no way reflects my beliefs about, or feelings and attitude toward, people of African American heritage."[22] While in one breath Spivey complained of being a victim of censorship based on the substance of disfavored remarks, in the next he asserted that his outburst had been little more than a verbal belch—rude, yes, but substantively meaningless.

The North Carolina Supreme Court affirmed Spivey's removal and in the course of doing so rebuffed his First Amendment challenge, ruling that his language was covered by that amendment's fighting-words exception. In *Chaplinsky v. New Hampshire,* the 1942 case that established the fighting-words doctrine, the United States Supreme Court observed, "There are certain well-defined and narrowly limited classes of speech, the prevention and punishment of which have never been thought to raise any constitutional problem. These include the lewd and obscene, the profane, the libelous, and the insulting or 'fighting' words—those which by their very utterance inflict injury or tend to incite an immediate breach of the peace."[23] Applying *Chaplinsky,* the North Carolina court ruled that Spivey's outburst had constituted a "classic" case of unprotected fighting words.[24] Elaborate hearings, the court maintained, were not needed to determine the effects of *nigger* on black targets. "No fact is more generally known," it declared, "than that a white man who calls a black man a 'nigger' within his hearing will hurt and anger the black man and often provoke him to confront the white man and retaliate."[25]

While the court ruled rightly in *Spivey,* there is good reason to reject the fighting-words doctrine on which its decision largely rested. Although *Chaplinsky* offers two bases on which language may be deemed fighting words, subsequent case law makes it clear that the primary and perhaps the exclusive grounds for declining to give First Amendment protection to so-called fighting words is that under certain circumstances, such language will either incite or be likely to incite an immediate breach of the peace by a target who responds impulsively and with violence. Thus, in a hypothetical dispute between an offensive speaker and a violent target, the fighting-words doctrine favors the target. Rather than insisting that the target of the speech control himself, the doctrine tells the offensive speaker to shut up. This is odd and objectionable. It allows "speech to be [regulated] . . . when directed at someone who would react violently to a verbal assault, but not [regulated] . . . when directed at someone with a more pacific bent."[26] It thus gives more leeway to insult a nun than a prize-fighter since the nun is presumably less likely to retaliate.[27] The fighting-words doctrine is in tension, moreover, with the dominant (and good) rule in criminal law that prevents "mere words standing alone . . . no matter how insulting, offensive, or abusive," from constituting the predicate for a provocation excuse.[28] In those jurisdictions that abide by the so-called mere-words doctrine (which we will examine further below), legal authority instructs everyone to exercise self-discipline even in the face of inflammatory taunts. The fighting-words doctrine weakens that salutary message.

In *Spivey,* the North Carolina Supreme Court wrote that the district attorney's "use of the word *nigger* . . . did not in any way involve an expression of his viewpoint on any local or national policy."[29] But clearly those who petitioned for his removal did believe that his utterance of the N-word revealed something—and something very disturbing—about his view of blacks. They would not have moved for his ouster had he merely called Jacobs, say, an asshole. That, too, would have been rude and abusive and indicative of a lack of self-discipline and decorum that would have reflected badly on the office of the district attorney. But *asshole* does not carry the ideological baggage that burdens the term *nigger*. During the United States presidential campaign of 2000, George W. Bush was overheard describing a reporter for the *New York Times* as "an asshole."[30] The incident raised a few eyebrows, to be sure, but it did not seem to cost him much, if anything, in public esteem. Had he been overheard describing a reporter (or anyone else) as a "nigger," however, his candidacy would have been doomed. That is because when whites use the word *nigger*, they are widely perceived to be showing their true colors as bigots. It is precisely because *nigger* is thought to indicate the presence of racist beliefs or sentiments that many people take such strong objection to it—as did the people who demanded Spivey's ouster.

The real reason and the better justification for Spivey's removal were that the statements he made rendered him unfit to fulfill his public responsibility. Such a responsibility entails a commitment to the idea that all people, regardless of race, should be treated equally and with respect before the bar of justice. By calling Ray Jacobs a nigger, Jerry Spivey cast a pall over public confidence in his commitment to accord all people due respect regardless of race.

In condemning officials or other leaders who use *nigger* or related terminology, we would do well to remember how complex people can be. Many unreconstructed white bigots have refrained from using the N-word even as they have continued to do everything in their power to hold blacks back.[31] At the same time, whites who use the N-word have made important contributions to the advancement of African Americans. Two politicians who come to mind here are Harry S Truman and Lyndon B. Johnson. Both used *nigger* in private conversation, and yet both surprised observers by taking unprecedented steps to elevate the fortunes of Negro Americans. Jerry Spivey's use of the N-word does not necessarily mean that he harbored racist views or would have failed to apply the law evenhandedly. Perhaps his remarks that night were an aberration. The problem is that his words raised justifiable doubts in the minds of North Carolinians, especially black North Carolinians, about whether he would or could treat all individuals equally, regardless of race. Spivey's misstep might have been reasonably overlooked or forgiven if he had occupied a position of lesser responsibility. But as the district attorney, he wielded massive and discretionary authority (it was up to him, for instance, to decide whether or not to seek capital punishment in a given case) that was effectively outside the scope of judicial review. In light of that power, and of the doubts raised regarding Spivey's ability to wield it effectively and fairly in the aftermath of his N-word incident, the North Carolina judiciary did just the right thing in removing him from office.[32]

The law of murder is a second area shadowed by *nigger*. Murder is the unjustified and intentional or reckless killing of a person. One way that society could signal that it abhors *nigger*-as-insult would be to deem justifiable the killing of anyone who insultingly deployed the epithet. No sensible person would seriously propose such a policy, of course, but what about excusing to some extent those who respond violently when provoked by the N-word?

That question has hovered in the background of several noteworthy cases. Consider the following episode, the basis for Richard Wright's short story "The Man Who Killed a Shadow."[33] On March 1, 1944, Julius Fisher, a black janitor at the National Cathedral in Washington, D.C., complained to a white librarian named Catherine Cooper Reardon about statements she had made to his boss regarding his poor performance on the job. She responded, he said, by calling him a "black nigger." He later testified that no white person had ever before spoken to him in this way. Angered, he slapped Reardon, who screamed. To stop her from screaming, he beat, choked, and stabbed her to death.[34]

At Fisher's trial for murder, his counsel, the redoubtable Charles Hamilton Houston—the great teacher of Thurgood Marshall—offered a defense of partial responsibility. While conceding that his client had killed the victim, Houston argued that he should be found guilty of second- as opposed to first-degree murder because he suffered from a mental deficiency. The difference in culpability amounted literally to a difference between life and death, since first-degree murder carried a mandatory death sentence, whereas second-degree murder carried a prison sentence of twenty years to life.

The trial judge allowed Houston to present evidence

intended to show that Fisher suffered from a diminished capacity to control himself and that Reardon had disastrously triggered this weakness by calling him a "black nigger." The judge refused, however, to instruct the jury that in reaching a decision it should consider evidence of the defendant's alleged mental deficiency. The jury convicted Fisher of first-degree murder. A court of appeals subsequently affirmed the trial judge's decision, as did, in its turn, the Supreme Court of the United States. Three justices dissented, maintaining that the trial judge had erred in refusing to instruct the jury specifically that it could consider Houston's theory of diminished capacity.

One of the dissenting justices was Felix Frankfurter, who, in an early draft of his dissent, suggested that "Miss Reardon's [reference to the defendant as a] 'black nigger' pulled the trigger that made the gun go off."[35] In the published version of the dissent, however, Frankfurter turned his attention from the specificity of the N-word as an incitement and instead focused on the defendant's deficiencies, observing that Fisher's "whole behavior seems that of a man of primitive emotions reacting to the stimulus of insult and proceeding from that point without purpose or design."[36]

Nearly a quarter of a century later, the N-word emerged as an important feature of another interracial killing in Washington. On June 4, 1968—two months after the assassination of Martin Luther King Jr. sparked major riots in the District of Columbia and throughout the country—Benjamin Murdock killed two white marines in a Little Tavern hamburger shop.[37] In the middle of a verbal altercation, one of the marines called Murdock a nigger, whereupon he drew a revolver and shot his antagonists. At trial, Murdock's attorney attempted to present a defense similar to the one Houston had mounted on Fisher's behalf. He argued that his client's "rotten social background" had contributed to a diminished capacity to control the rage that exploded when the marine referred to him and his buddies as niggers. The trial judge, however, instructed the jury to disregard the "rotten social background" defense, whereupon the jury convicted Murdock of second-degree murder. [38]

In neither Fisher's nor Murdock's case did the defense lawyer argue that the jury ought to be instructed that the word *nigger* alone could be such a powerful incitement to violence that it should be deemed a provocation sufficient to reduce the defendant's crime from murder to manslaughter. Every jurisdiction in the United States allows a murder defendant to claim, under certain conditions, that his killing of another was sufficiently provoked that his crime should be demoted from murder—the acme of all crimes against persons—to manslaughter, a lesser (albeit still serious) offense. The question that could have been posed in both *Fisher* and *Murdock* was whether being called a nigger constituted a circumstance that might allow a defendant to claim that the provocation had been such that he had lost control of himself, killed in the heat of passion, and therefore committed a crime that, though terrible, was nonetheless less morally condemnable than a killing done in cold blood. The likely reason that the two men's lawyers refrained from pressing the question is that in Washington in those years—and the same is true today[39]—the mere-words doctrine was well-established law.

That doctrine would be squarely confronted in *State of*

North Carolina v. Rufus Coley Watson, Jr., a 1975 case in which a black inmate in a corrections facility killed a white inmate over his use of the word *nigger*.[40] At trial, Watson's attorney argued that in view of the verbal provocation the defendant had faced, the jury should at least be given instructions that would permit it to consider whether he had committed manslaughter rather than murder. The trial judge, however, thwarted that strategy by instructing the jury that "Words and gestures alone[,] . . . regardless of how insulting or inflammatory those words or gestures may be, do not constitute adequate provocation for the taking of human life."[41] The jury convicted Watson of second-degree murder.

On appeal, the defense counsel sought to oust the mere-words doctrine as the governing law. In asserting his position, he cited as precedent an early-nineteenth-century case in which a white man named Tackett had been charged with murdering a black slave named Daniel.[42] There was enmity between the two men because Tackett had made sexual overtures toward Daniel's wife, a free woman of color. Tackett wanted to offer evidence that Daniel had been a turbulent man, impudent and insolent to white people. He argued that this fact in itself should allow a jury to reduce his crime from murder to manslaughter. The judge excluded the proposed testimony, ruling that the defendant's argument could be predicated only upon evidence that the deceased slave had been impudent and insolent to Tackett himself. A jury convicted Tackett and sentenced him to death.

The North Carolina Supreme Court, ruling on Tackett's appeal, held that the trial judge should have allowed the defen-

dant to present evidence regarding Daniel's general comport-
ment around whites. The trial judge's fundamental mistake,
according to Chief Justice Taylor, had consisted in his erroneous belief that "the case was to be determined by the same
rules and principles of law as if the deceased had been a white
man."[43] The law of provocation in antebellum North Carolina
had thus served to cheapen the lives of black slaves who failed
to be properly deferential to whites. One hundred fifty-five
years later, in *Watson*, the defense counsel tried to turn the
same ruling around to mitigate his (black) client's actions. But
the North Carolina Supreme Court would have none of it.
Instead, it indicated that its earlier, racially discriminatory
conception of provocation was long dead and had been superseded by a clear, clean rule that applied to all: no mere words
could provide any degree of excuse warranting a lessening of
punishment for the taking of another's life.

That rule is law throughout much, though by no means all,
of the United States. Several states, including California, permit juries to consider the provocation excuse whenever the
evidence points to any circumstances, including mere words
or gestures, that might cause a reasonable person to lose control over himself or herself. But a majority of the states still
embrace the rule that words alone cannot constitute provocation sufficient to diminish murder to manslaughter.

Is the mere-words doctrine a good rule in light of everything we know about the turmoil, distress, and rage that
nigger-as-insult can generate within its targets?[44] An argument
for reform might begin with the proposition that *nigger* and
similar slurs are not mere words. Professor Charles Lawrence

has described them as "assaultive" and classified them as "a form of violence by speech" that causes a target to feel as though he or she had been slapped in the face.[45] Professor Richard Delgado similarly refers to such speech as "words that wound."[46] The likening of racist speech to violence is significant in this context because violence is universally recognized as creating a predicate for a provocation excuse. If calling someone a nigger is indeed a "form of violence by speech," then it seems reasonable that at least in some circumstances, the N-word should be deemed a provocation in the eyes of the law.

An argument against this reform is that black people can and do routinely show discipline, intelligence, and productiveness even in the face of *nigger,* and that the law should undergird such conduct by offering no excuse to those who react with violence. People who hold this view may fear what Professor Ann Coughlin has termed "the perils of leniency,"[47] believing that a modification of the mere-words doctrine out of concern over the *nigger* insult will result in an entrenchment of the notion that blacks are less capable of self-control than others and ought, on that account, to be forgiven for their putatively unavoidable impulsiveness.

Adherents to this view can take inspiration from Ralph Ellison. There is an American Negro tradition, he wrote, "which teaches one to deflect racial provocation and to master and contain pain. It is a tradition which abhors as obscene any trading on one's own anguish for gain or sympathy; which springs not from a desire to deny the harshness of existence but from a will to deal with it as men at their best have always done."[48]

The issue is agonizingly close, with strong arguments on both sides. One's conclusion turns largely on one's belief regarding the primary purpose of criminal law. If the primary purpose is utilitarian crime control, the mere-words doctrine should be retained. If the primary purpose of the criminal law is retribution—dishing out just deserts—reform of the mere-word doctrine is preferable. An ambivalent retributivist, I choose the latter alternative. I am persuaded that there should be no bright-line limits to the array of provocations that a jury is permitted to consider for the purposes of mitigation. It should be up to a jury to determine whether, in fact, a defendant lost control of himself or herself in the face of *nigger* or any other alleged provocation and whether society should soften its punishment in the event of such a loss of control.[49]

The third category of *nigger* litigation is composed of cases in which targets of the slur have invoked tort law or antidiscrimination law to sue their tormentors.

Many jurisdictions offer individuals the possibility of obtaining relief for what tort law terms "the intentional infliction of emotional distress."[50] This legal weapon emerged from the notion that under certain circumstances, even in the absence of offensive touching or threats of force, some conduct may be so outrageous that a formal means of redress should be available to offended parties. Successful applications of this idea in its early years involved malevolent practical jokes, as in the case of a plaintiff who was told that her husband had been severely injured, while the defendant knew that he was in fact safe.[51] Other scenarios that have given rise to successful lawsuits include instances of a defendant's spreading false rumors that a plaintiff's son had hanged himself,[52] a defendant's bringing a mob to a plaintiff's door at night and voicing a threat to lynch him unless he left town,[53] and a defendant's telephoning the plaintiff around the clock seeking repayment of a debt.[54] The jurisprudence of emotional distress also contains a body of precedent related to *nigger*. Consider the following cases: *Wiggs v. Courshon*[55] and *Nims v. Harrison*.[56]

Wiggs involved black customers at a motel restaurant in Miami, Florida, who became embroiled in an argument with a waitress over a food order. Among these customers were several adults and one seven-year-old boy. At one point in the dispute, the waitress exclaimed to one of the adults, "You can't talk to me like that, you black son of a bitch. I will kill you."[57] Later, outside of the immediate presence of the plaintiffs but within earshot of them, the waitress shouted, "They are nothing but a bunch of niggers."[58] The plaintiffs immediately checked out of the motel. The next day, when they returned to tell a manager what had happened, they were advised, "You shouldn't feel so bad. . . . [That waitress] is prejudiced against Catholics, Jews, and all other kinds of minorities."[59] Upset, the plaintiffs cut short their vacation, went home, and eventually sued, persevering through trial to win a jury verdict.

The plaintiff in *Harrison* was a black high school teacher, Rosalind Nims, who sued several graduating students because of the nature of comments about and threats toward her that they published in a newsletter distributed at the school. The newsletter described Nims as the "most fucked-up teacher," assailed her as "a stupid bitch . . . who has black skin and is a fucking gigaboo [*sic*]," and contained the declarations "I will kill you you fucking whore" and "I will rape you and all of your children and cousins you stupid motherfucking bitch." For good measure, the writer added, "Die nigger."[60]

Nims charged the students responsible with intentional infliction of emotional distress and sued for damages. A trial court judge dismissed the complaint, ruling that even if the facts alleged by the plaintiff were true, they failed as a matter of law to reach the level of outrageousness required for a recovery of damages. An appellate court reversed, concluding that "justice, reason and common sense compel a remedy for the revilement inflicted upon the teacher . . . provided that the facts alleged are proven." The Florida Court of Appeal found that the conduct alleged "is so outrageous in character, and so extreme in degree, as to go beyond all possible bounds of decency; it is utterly intolerable in a civilized community."[61]

While these cases demonstrate that it is possible to recover in tort for racial insults, imposing difficulties lie in wait for those who attempt to do so. First, seeking redress through litigation is typically expensive, nerve-racking, fatiguing, and time-consuming. Second, the formal requirements of the tort of intentional infliction of emotional distress are daunting. Plaintiffs must show that the offending conduct was extreme and outrageous; that it was intentional or reckless; that it caused emotional distress; and that the emotional distress caused was severe. According to the American Law Institute:

It has not been enough that the defendant has acted
with an intent which is tortious or even criminal, or that
he has intended to inflict emotional distress, or even that
his conduct has been characterized by "malice," or a
degree of aggravation which would entitle the plaintiff to
punitive damages for another tort. Liability has been
found only where the conduct has been so outrageous in
character, and so extreme in degree, as to go beyond all
possible bounds of decency, and to be regarded as atro-
cious, and utterly intolerable in a civilized community.
Generally, the case is one in which the recitation of the
facts to an average member of the community would
arouse his resentment against the actor and lead him to
exclaim, "Outrageous!"[62]

Third, many judges have been reluctant to permit damage
awards based on claims of emotional distress caused solely or
even primarily by verbal abuse. They fear trumped-up charges
and injuries. They fear infringements upon liberty in general
and, more particularly, upon that guaranteed by the First
Amendment to the United States Constitution. They also fear
encouraging a debilitating oversensitivity and an overdepen-
dence on courts. Scores of judges embrace the proposition
that "against a large part of the frictions and irritations and
clashing of temperaments incident to participation in a community life, a certain toughening of the mental hide is a better
protection than the law could ever be."[63] This attitude is mir-
rored in many judicial decisions. In *Wiggs*, for example—the
case of the foulmouthed waitress—the plaintiffs prevailed,

but that did not prevent the judge from intervening to lower the damage award. After the jury awarded $25,000 in damages, the trial judge stated that he would order a new trial unless the plaintiffs accepted a lesser sum. According to the judge, the jury had "plainly embarked on a giveaway program far out of line with common sense and experience."[64] While he condemned "the uncivil outburst and rude remarks made by [the restaurant] waitress," he concluded that "a line would quickly form by members of any ethnic group to receive $25,000 as balm for an ethnic or racial epithet."[65] To prevent the plaintiffs from reaping what he perceived as a windfall, he reduced the money damages to one-tenth of the amount awarded by the jury, or $2,500.

In other instances, judges have not even allowed juries to decide the matter. Consider the following episodes:

A lawyer twice called a young black man a nigger while trying to collect on a debt. When the target of the insult sued, the trial judge granted summary judgment in favor of the defendant. He was upheld by the Kansas Court of Appeals, which ruled, "It appears to us that the trial judge was fully justified in regarding the epithets as 'mere insults' of the kind which must be tolerated in our rough-edged society."[66]

A black man went to a store to return merchandise that he believed to be subpar. As a precondition for giving him a refund, a sales clerk insisted that the man sign a sales slip on which was written the notation "Arrogant nigger refused exchange—says he doesn't like products." Courts in Illinois ruled that the notation, albeit rude, was insufficiently extreme and outrageous to serve as a predicate for the plaintiff's lawsuit.[67]

An employee in a Zayre's department store called a customer a nigger during a dispute over goods. When the customer subsequently sued, a judge ruled that even if the defendant had in fact said what the plaintiff alleged she had said, that conduct, though offensive, did not reach the level of outrageousness required for a recovery. Insulting and abusive though *nigger* might be, the court observed, "taken in this context it does not amount to the type of extreme and outrageous conduct which gives rise to a cause of action. Clearly the law cannot serve to redress all indignities."[68]

A black man alleged that a white bartender had referred to him angrily as a nigger when he saw him speaking to some white women seated at the bar. When the man sued for damages, a judge granted summary judgment to the defendant. While referring to a person as a nigger was indeed outrageous, the court declared, the defendant should nonetheless prevail because the plaintiff had failed to show to the satisfaction of the court that his distress was severe.[69]

An employee responsible for looking after parking spaces called a person "nigger" in the course of an argument over a space. When the insulted party sued, the court ruled in favor of the defendant, essentially reasoning that the conduct complained of, albeit regrettable, had not been so bad and injurious as to warrant legal interference.[70]

An employee sued a supervisor who had referred to him as a "sleazy nigger." A judge disallowed the claim for intentional infliction of emotional distress on the grounds that the remark did not rise to the level of intolerable conduct. Affirming the trial judge, an appellate panel commented that "as part of living in our society, we must tolerate a certain amount of offensive expression."[71]

A plaintiff alleged that his employer had called him a "stupid nigger" and a "token nigger" and proclaimed that the firm "would never pay a nigger $75,000 a year." Noting that "rarely will conduct in the employment context rise to the level of outrageousness necessary to establish a basis of recovery for intentional infliction of emotional distress," the trial judge dismissed this aspect of the plaintiff's suit. The alleged statements were "inconsiderate," the judge conceded, but they did not, he said, rise to the level of outrageousness the law required.[72]

Statutes prohibiting racial discrimination in employment provide yet another means by which the law offers recourse to targets of *nigger*. The most widely used of these statutes is Title VII of the Civil Rights Act of 1964. Two questions typically confront Title VII plaintiffs in suits involving *nigger*. The first arises in situations in which a plaintiff complains that his or her race has prompted an adverse decision regarding hire, promotion, or term of employment. In such cases, the question is whether a decision maker's use of the word *nigger* provides direct evidence of racial discrimination. The second question arises in situations in which a plaintiff charges that use of the N-word in the workplace has created a hostile work environment. Here the key issue is often whether such usage has been sufficiently burdensome that the legal system ought to make relief available. Consider the following cases, which illustrate these two scenarios.

In 1967 Henry Brown, a black man, got a job as a janitor with the East Mississippi Electric Power Association (EMEPA). Over the years he won promotions within the company, eventually attaining the position of serviceman, a post in which he performed such tasks as installing meters, pulling meters, troubleshooting in instances of malfunction, and, occasionally, collecting on overdue accounts. Servicemen work alone and enjoy a degree of independence that other EMEPA employees do not have. Brown was the company's first African American serviceman.

In 1989, EMEPA higher-ups informed Brown that he would have to either accept reassignment or else leave the company. His supervisors maintained that their action was prompted by complaints from customers, several of whom had asserted that Brown was rude and had cursed at them. One had charged that he engaged in reckless driving. The complaints had continued even after Brown had received an earlier warning to avoid consumer dissatisfaction. Faced with a choice between reassignment (and therefore the loss of his post as a serviceman) and termination, Brown ceased working for EMEPA and thereafter sued, charging that the company had subjected him to racial discrimination. According to Brown, EMEPA treated him differently, more harshly, than it did its white servicemen. Under similar circumstances, he averred, a white serviceman would not even have been reprimanded, much less demoted.[73]

As a key piece of evidence in his case, Brown cited a supervisor's use of *nigger*. In 1985, prior to becoming a serviceman,

Brown had overheard an EMEPA supervisor on the radio discussing a traffic accident. At some point in the conversation, he testified, the supervisor said something to the effect of, he felt like getting a gun and shooting the offending "nigger." A couple of months later, after he became a serviceman, Brown heard this same supervisor say to another serviceman, "You should have hooked that power up for that nigger [presumably a customer]. You know how they are." According to Brown, he complained about this use of the N-word to a company official, who told him he would take care of the problem. A while later, however, the supervisor called him into his office and demanded that he stop calling him by his first name over the company radio. "If you call me [by my first name] one more time on that radio," the supervisor threatened, "I'll call you 'nigger.' " Brown said he subsequently overheard the same supervisor referring to him as a nigger on two occasions. In one instance the supervisor said, "Look at my little nigger going down the hall. We brung him to his knees." At another time he declared, "We finally got what we wanted. We got rid of that little nigger."

That the supervisor occasionally used the N-word was uncontested; other EMEPA employees, including several whites, confirmed this. And the supervisor himself admitted that *nigger* was part of his vocabulary. He insisted, though, that he did not use the word in front of blacks and that he had largely stopped saying "nigger" after company officials instructed him to do so.

After a trial, United States District Court Judge Tom S. Lee ruled in favor of EMEPA. He gave several reasons for his decision. Contrary to what Brown alleged, he said, white service-men *had* been reprimanded following customer complaints; one had even been fired. Then, too, Brown had offered no evidence to show that the company condoned the use of racial slurs. After the serviceman complained to company officials about the supervisor's use of the N-word, they responded by telling the supervisor to stop doing it or risk being fired. The judge disbelieved Brown's testimony regarding the supervisor's alleged continued use of the N-word after that warning and expressly credited the supervisor's denial that he had referred to Brown as a "little nigger." The judge noted that it was this very supervisor who had been instrumental in getting Brown promoted to the position of serviceman in the first place. Judge Lee stressed, moreover, that in the final confrontation between Brown and company officials, it was the supervisor who had sought to intervene on Brown's behalf and implored him to cool off before quitting and thus throwing away the benefits he had accrued over twenty years of employment at EMEPA.

The Fifth Circuit Court of Appeals reversed Judge Lee. It ruled that the supervisor's "routine use of racial slurs constitutes direct evidence that racial animus was a motivating factor in the contested disciplinary decisions."[74] According to the appellate judges, the supervisor's repeated use of *nigger* could not be dismissed as an innocent habit: "Unlike certain age-related comments [e.g., 'young tigers'] which we have found too vague to constitute evidence of discrimination, the term *nigger* is a universally recognized opprobrium, stigmatizing African-Americans because of their race. That [the supervisor]

73

usually was circumspect in using the term in the presence of African-Americans underscores that he knew it was insulting. Nonetheless, he persisted in demeaning African-Americans by using it among whites. This is racism."[75] Concluding that this individual's racism had infected the decision to reassign and demote Brown, the court of appeals asserted that the supervisor's " 'I had to dust my little nigger' comment . . . demonstrates that his racism distorted Brown's employment record and extended to decisions of the type at bar."[76] Furthermore, the appeals court took the unusual step of deciding key factual issues of the sort that are typically remanded to the trial judge for determination. When a plaintiff shows that racial bias played a role in a challenged decision, for example, the defendant is offered the opportunity to show that he would have made the same decision even absent the racial bias. Usually trial courts make such findings. In this case, however, the court of appeals decided the issue on its own, circumventing the trial judge—purportedly out of "a prudential concern for scarce judicial resources."[77]

Mr. Brown was very lucky; other appellate courts might well have decided the case differently. For one thing, appellate courts generally defer to the factual findings of trial judges. But in this case—though without expressly saying so—the appeals court declined to accept Judge Lee's findings of fact. Whereas Judge Lee had explicitly discredited Brown's testimony about hearing the supervisor refer to him as a "little nigger," the appellate court cited this very testimony as the predicate for its conclusions that the supervisor was racially biased and had contaminated EMEPA's decision making with his prejudice.

The probable mainsprings of the decision in *Brown* were an appreciation of the likelihood that extraordinary scrutiny had been focused upon EMEPA's first black serviceman; a realistic sense that he was bound to receive more than his fair share of white customer complaints regardless of his actual conduct; distrust of the trial judge's perception of the situation; and, outweighing any other single consideration, a deep reluctance to rule in favor of a white employer whose place of business echoed with *nigger* references. "At the heart of this appeal," the appellate court declared, "is the significance of [the supervisor's] routine use of the term *nigger*."[78] Contradicting the defendant's dismissal of such language as "isolated remarks," the plaintiff had succeeded in persuading the appellate court that the supervisor's use of *nigger* constituted "direct evidence" of illegal racial discrimination. Direct evidence is evidence that, if believed, proves a fact without inference or presumption. It precludes the necessity of inferring whether a challenged action constitutes (in this context) racial discrimination, because it *compels* that conclusion.

Given the protean character of *nigger,* which may signal several different (even contradictory) meanings, it is probably erroneous to conclude that the word itself *necessarily* furnishes proof of racial discrimination, even when the speaker is white and the target black. Automatic labeling of *nigger* may be an efficient shorthand method for judicially assessing the N-word—a method whose inevitable mistakes may be tolerable given the savings it affords in labor and time. Perhaps in the context of antidiscrimination law at the workplace, moreover, it is better to err on the side of overenforcement rather than underenforcement. Still, even if that is so, it is important to remember that the N-word is not self-defining. Its actual meaning in any given instance always depends on surrounding circumstances. Deriving an understanding of *nigger* thus always requires interpretation.

The second category of Title VII cases featuring *nigger* comprises lawsuits alleging that an employer has either knowingly or negligently condoned a racially hostile workplace environment. One such suit was filed by James H. Spriggs, an African American who worked at the Diamond Auto Glass Company in Forestville, Maryland, as a customer service representative in the 1990s.[79] Spriggs left Diamond because of what he viewed as the company's inadequate response to misconduct on the part of his supervisor, a white man named Ernest Stickell. According to Spriggs, Stickell, in his presence, constantly referred to African American customers and employees as monkeys and niggers. Stickell himself was married to a black woman, but according to Spriggs, she, too, was subjected to her husband's racial vilification. Stickell referred to her as a black bitch and directed racial slurs at her in agitated phone conversations that Spriggs said he could not help but overhear. Angered, Spriggs quit Diamond but returned after the company's management assured him it would force Stickell to clean up his language. Spriggs maintained, however, that Diamond failed to make good on its promise and that Stickell's verbal conduct did not improve; indeed, in Spriggs's view, his supervisor's behavior worsened. Stickell continued to describe his wife in racially derogatory terms and repeatedly called Spriggs a monkey and a nigger to his face. Spriggs claimed that Stickell also inserted between pages of a manual that he (Spriggs) regularly consulted a picture of a monkey, with a notation that read, "So you'll never forget who you are."[80]

Spriggs eventually resigned and sued, charging that he had been victimized by harassment that created a racially hostile workplace in violation of Title VII. In order to prevail, he would have to satisfy both a subjective and an objective requirement: he needed to show that he himself had actually perceived the work environment to be abusive and that a reasonable person would also view it thus.[81] According to the Supreme Court, "Conduct that is not severe or pervasive enough to create an objectively hostile or abusive work environment . . . is beyond Title VII's purview."[82] The "mere utterance of an . . . epithet which engenders offensive feelings in an employee" is insufficient grounds;[83] the conduct objected to must be sufficiently bad that "a reasonable person" would find it to be intolerably hostile. Many judges demand that "reasonable people" be thick-skinned and have a high threshold for tolerating irksome, even deplorable, conduct. Spriggs drew such a judge. United States District Court Judge Frederic N. Smalkin granted summary judgment to Diamond, holding that, even assuming that his factual allegations were accurate, Spriggs's suit failed as a matter of law. But the Fourth Circuit Court of Appeals reversed, remanding the case for trial. The appellate court concluded that the language Spriggs had found objectionable was sufficiently injurious to be deemed a violation of Title VII if, upon trial, his allegations were determined to be true. Central to the court's ruling was the special place of *nigger* in the lexicon of verbal abuse. "Perhaps no single act," the court remarked, "can more quickly alter the conditions of employment and create an abusive working environment than the use of . . . 'nigger' by a supervisor in the presence of his subordinates."[84] Elaborating, the court averred that "far more than a 'mere offensive utterance,' the word 'nigger' is pure anathema to African-Americans."[85]

Hostile-workplace litigation—like every other kind—is frustrating, expensive, and risky. Corporate employers are liable for abuse committed by their employees, but only if they are put on notice that such abuse is occurring. This poses a dilemma for victims. If they repeatedly report abusive behavior by coworkers, they may improve their chances of obtaining legal relief in the event of litigation, but they also run the risk of poisoning relations with colleagues and alienating supervisors. Compounding this conundrum is the difficulty of predicting whether or not a court will see the reported misconduct as unlawful. No bright line authoritatively distinguishes mere rudeness from illegal abuse; drawing the line is a matter of judgment, and judgments vary.

Consider the plight of James L. Bolden Jr., an African American who worked as an electrician for eight years for PRC, Inc. Long tormented by his coworkers, Bolden finally quit and sued his employer. He alleged that his coworkers had constantly called him "faggot," "fool," "dickhead," and "dumbshit"; that one coworker had walked over to his work area and farted directly at him; that several others had said "nigger" in his presence; and that on one occasion a colleague had warned, "You better be careful because we know people in [the] Ku Klux Klan."[86]

A federal district judge, affirmed by a court of appeals, ruled that even if Bolden's allegations were accurate, they failed as a matter of law to constitute the predicate for a hostile-work-environment claim. While the judges acknowledged that the racial abuse alleged was deplorable, they found that it was insufficiently deplorable to trigger the remedies contained in Title VII. Echoing established doctrine, the judges declared that a plaintiff must prove more than the occurrence of "a few isolated incidents of racial enmity" or the utterance of "sporadic racial slurs."[87] What a plaintiff needed to show, they suggested, was "a steady barrage of opprobrious racial comments."[88] In the judges' view, Bolden's complaints fell far short of this threshold. "The blatant racial harassment," they pointed out, "came from only two of his co-workers on a couple of occasions," and the "racial jokes and slurs were infrequent."[89]

The appellate judges who affirmed dismissal erred in ruling that, as a matter of law, no reasonable juror could find for Bolden based on the evidence he presented. They saw a wholly one-sided case when they should have seen a more complicated controversy. The evidence was such that reasonable jurors could have disagreed—meaning that the judges should have permitted a jury to resolve the dispute.

In light of the outcome in Bolden's case, can a plaintiff successfully sue if he or she is referred to "only" once with hostility as a nigger? How about twice? Or three times? At what point does race-baiting on the job become illegal? The only way to answer such questions sensibly is in terms of probabilities, taking into account such considerations as where a lawsuit is filed and before which judge the suit will be heard.[90] While certain judges stress that episodic misconduct is usually insufficient to support a hostile-work-environment claim, others make rulings and generate rhetoric friendlier to plaintiffs, including the observation that "even a single episode of harassment, if severe enough, can establish a hostile work environment."[91]

Linda Jackson's fate, like Bolden's, exemplifies the variability of different listeners' assessments of *nigger* even in the context of federal statutory law. Jackson sued the Quanex Corporation of Detroit, Michigan, alleging that it fostered a racially hostile work environment.[92] To make her case, she introduced evidence that racial slurring insulting to blacks was rife in the workplace. She testified, for example, that at a staff meeting a superior stated, "We are up to our asses in nigger sludge."[93] Jackson also introduced evidence that racist graffiti was prevalent and that white workers constantly attempted to sabotage or otherwise injure their black colleagues. In one incident, a fellow worker had called Jackson a nigger bitch and physically assaulted her. In the aftermath, *both* workers had been suspended for three days, and Jackson had been denied the opportunity to work overtime.

United States District Court Judge Avern Cohn disposed of Jackson's case by granting judgment to the defendant. He found that in some instances the company had not been notified of objectionable conditions and that in others management had responded adequately. Judge Cohn also stressed that several of the racist acts that Jackson had entered into evidence either had not occurred in her presence or had not been directed at her, and that several of the actions she was objecting to were so commonplace at Quanex as to have become "conventional conditions on the factory floor."[94]

A federal court of appeals reversed Judge Cohn in an unusually harsh ruling that branded his view of the relevant law and facts as "myopic." According to the appellate court, Judge Cohn had erroneously chopped the evidence into unconnected bits that robbed the plaintiff of a fair chance to show that, in their accumulated totality, the individual episodes and incidents constituted an ugly portrait of intolerable racial hostility. Unlike the trial judge, the appellate judges deemed the defendants' reactions to racism on the factory floor to be both tardy and deficient, insofar as management had made no effort whatsoever to discover the identity of those behind the graffiti. And unlike the trial judge, the appellate judges focused not on what had been reported to management by victims but instead on what management actually knew or should have known about racial abuse among its workers. Finally, the appellate court took strong exception to what it saw as "potentially the most disturbing" aspect of Judge Cohn's ruling: the "decision to minimize proof of persistent racial slurs and graffiti at Quanex" on the grounds that their very prevalence made them less rather than more problematic as a legal matter. Averring that Judge Cohn's reasoning reflected an unseemly class bias that would impose lower demands on blue-collar than on white-collar worksites, the appellate judges "squarely denounce[d] the notion that increasing regularity of racial slurs and graffiti renders such conduct acceptable, normal, or part of 'conventional conditions on the factory floor.' "[95]

Were the appellate judges correct with respect to this last point? Yes, they were. It would have been a mistake to have offered safe harbor to racially abusive language because such language was pervasive and customary at a given worksite. To have done so would have encouraged inertia when clearly the express aim of Title VII and similar statutes is to uproot racist custom.[96] This was not a case in which a defendant was contesting whether a particular usage of *nigger* should be deemed insulting; here that was conceded. Rather, the defendant in Jackson's case was arguing that, given the facts she alleged, and given the law of Title VII, no juror could reasonably conclude the plaintiff had been subjected to racial harassment that was sufficiently bad to warrant legal relief. That is an argument that the defendant rightly lost.

A fourth setting in which *nigger* arises as a focal point in litigation involves cases in which the judge must decide whether certain evidence that one party wants to offer to the jury should be admitted. The party seeking to exclude the evidence from the trial argues that it is more prejudicial than probative—or in layman's terms, more likely to impede than to advance the search for truth, in that its inclusion is inessential to a sound adjudication of the facts in dispute and will poison the minds of the jurors, making them unable to attend fairly to their task. Examples abound of *nigger* in this context.

Michael Brad Magleby, for instance, was charged with committing crimes in connection with burning a cross on the property of an interracial family. During the trial, over defense counsel's objections, prosecutors read lyrics of a song that Magleby was said to have listened to on the evening of the cross burning. The lyrics featured numerous references to *nigger,* as in "Nigger, nigger, get out of here."[97] A court of appeals upheld Magleby's conviction, holding that the trial judge had not abused his discretion by admitting the song lyrics into evidence.

In another case, Jack William Tocco was prosecuted for racketeering. During his trial, prosecutors played taped conversations for the jury in which the defendant and a close associate could be heard saying, among other things, that they "might win up here [in Detroit] with a nigger trial, nigger jury."[98] While agreeing with the defendant that "those particular denigrating comments were unfairly prejudicial," an appellate court affirmed his conviction because the prejudicial comments constituted only a small portion of the captured discussion, and other evidence also pointed to his guilt.[99]

The issue surfaces in civil as well as criminal cases. Aleia Robinson sued the United States Postal Service for violating Title VII of the Civil Rights Act by discriminating against her on racial grounds. At trial she sought to introduce into evidence a document entitled "Nigger Employment Application," which in her view supported her contention that racism was pervasive at the Cincinnati, Ohio, facility where she worked. A parody of a standard employment application, this document listed as possible choices for birthplace the zoo, a cotton field, a back alley, and an animal hospital. Robinson stated that she was prepared to present witnesses who would testify that the parody had been widely circulated at her workplace, that no one had ever been disciplined in connection with it, and that it had prompted nothing more than laughter on the part of several supervisors. A magistrate judge excluded the application from evidence, declaring that it was irrelevant to the legal issues in question and would be more prejudicial than probative in resolving the dispute. A court of appeals disagreed, finding that the magistrate judge's evidentiary ruling had been overly restrictive. Robinson was awarded a new trial.[100]

In a suit charging police officers with using excessive force in making a lawful arrest, a judge excluded from evidence a portion of a tape recorded during the incident in question. The excluded portion would have revealed that an arresting officer shouted at one point, "Did you get that nigger?"[101] A court of appeals reversed and granted the plaintiff a new trial. Exasperated, the appellate tribunal declared, "It is difficult to understand why [the trial judge] believed that all of the words uttered at the time of the arrest and beating were probative and helpful to the task the jury faced, except the phrase containing the word 'nigger.' . . . Because the district court did not state for the record any reason for excluding this evidence, and neither the parties nor this court can discern any reason for its exclusion, we hold that the district court abused its discretion."[102]

Of course, the most famous evidentiary ruling involving the N-word came in response to efforts to bring a witness's use of the term to the attention of the jury in the murder trial of O. J. Simpson.[103] In that case, Simpson was charged with murdering his former wife Nicole Brown Simpson and an acquaintance of hers named Ronald Goldman. The police had allegedly found incriminating evidence at the murder site and at Simpson's residence, including a bloody glove presumably worn by the murderer. Simpson's attorneys maintained that the bloody glove had been planted by police officer Mark Fuhrman.

The prosecutors requested that the presiding judge, Lance Ito, prevent defense counsel from questioning Fuhrman with regard to his racial attitudes, including his alleged penchant for derogatorily referring to blacks as niggers. The title of the prosecution's motion—"People's Motion . . . to Exclude from Trial Remote, Inflammatory, and Irrelevant Character Evidence regarding L.A.P.D. Detective Mark Fuhrman"— revealed its essential argument. Pleading for the judge to exclude any inquiry into Fuhrman's linguistic habits, prosecutor Christopher Darden declared that because the N-word "is the filthiest, dirtiest, nastiest word in the English language," references to it "will blind the jury. It will blind them to the truth. . . . It will affect their judgment. It will impair their ability to be fair and impartial. . . . If you allow [the defense] to use their word and play this race card, not only [do] the direction and the focus of the case change, but the entire complexion of the case changes. It is a race case then. It is white versus black, African American versus Caucasian, us versus them, us versus the system."[104]

The defense responded with a dual argument. First, it maintained that evidence relating to Fuhrman's racial views was relevant to its theory that for reasons of racial animus, the officer had planted evidence. Second, it derided the notion that testimony regarding Fuhrman's use of the word *nigger* would prevent jurors from sensibly evaluating the evidence at hand. It was "demeaning," defense counsel Johnny Cochran argued, to suggest that black jurors—"African Americans [whose forebears] have lived under oppression for two hundred–plus years in this country," and who themselves had lived with "offensive words, offensive looks, [and] offensive treatment every day of their lives"—would be unable to deliberate fairly if they were made aware of a witness's racial views, as evidenced in part by his usage of the N-word.[105]

Judge Ito rightly decided to permit Simpson's attorneys to ask Fuhrman whether, over the preceding ten years, he had ever used the N-word. Fuhrman denied that he had—a statement that, instead of ending the matter, set the stage for a second controversy. Several months after Fuhrman's denial, audiotapes were discovered on which he was heard using the N-word repeatedly and with relish. The defense attorneys, not surprisingly, sought to introduce this new evidence in its entirety. The prosecution, for its part, sought to prevent or at least to minimize the jury's exposure to the tapes. Judge Ito compromised: he permitted the jury to hear Fuhrman say "nigger" twice and also allowed the defense to elicit an acknowledgment that in the taped conversations he used the N-word some forty-one times. The jury subsequently acquitted Simpson, in perhaps the most hotly debated jury verdict in American legal history.

Like every other significant feature of American life—including cigarettes, guns, pornography, drugs, stock trading, sex, religion, and money—*nigger* is thoroughly enmeshed in litigation. The disorderly diversity of the conflicts in which it figures is remarkable. The following three cases illustrate that variety.

Otis Ross successfully sued the Douglas County, Nebraska, correctional facility for violating federal antidiscrimination law. Ross, a black prison guard, complained of being subjected to a constant barrage of abuse by a supervisor who addressed him as "nigger" and "black boy" and referred to Ross's white wife as "whitey." The abusive supervisor was also black. The county posited that as a matter of law, blacks could not subject other blacks to a racially hostile workplace. The judges, however, wisely rejected that argument, quoting Thurgood Marshall's observation that given the mysteries of human motivation, "it would be unwise to presume as a matter of law that human beings of one definable group will not discriminate against other members of their group."[106]

In a second case, a white woman sued for and won a divorce after forty years of marriage and three children. She alleged that her husband had subjected her to cruel and inhuman treatment due to his rage at their daughter's decision to marry someone whom the court described as "a gentleman of Puerto Rican descent." The husband had refused to attend the wedding and would not speak to his daughter or acknowledge his son-in-law. Infuriated by his wife's acceptance of the marriage, he told her that her presence made him feel like puking. For good measure, he repeatedly called her a nigger lover.[107]

A third memorable case arose from one man's efforts to effectuate Lenny Bruce's strategy to defang *nigger* through continuous use. Russell Lawrence Lee petitioned a court to change his name to "Mister Nigger."[108] His intention in doing this, he wrote, was to "steal the stinging degradation—the thunder, the wrath, the shame and racial slur—from the word *nigger*."[109] A trial court, affirmed by the California Court of Appeals, rejected his petition. The appellate court maintained that while the petitioner had a common-law right to use whatever name he chose, the judiciary did not have to assist him in his experiment and could, in this instance, properly refrain from doing so, since the "proposed surname is commonly considered to be a racial epithet and has the potential to be a 'fighting word.' "[110]

These three cases, unusual though they all are, nonetheless represent a type of conflict that judges will continue to face. For *nigger* and its variants will keep showing up in court so long as they remain key words that tap into and reflect powerful emotions. For the forseeable future, at least, *nigger* will constitute a peculiar, resilient, ever-changing fixture in the American jurisprudence of epithets.

CHAPTER THREE

Pitfalls in Fighting *Nigger:*
Perils of Deception, Censoriousness,
and Excessive Anger

After the Civil War, a former master approached a former slave while she was tending livestock. "What you doin', nigger?" he asked, as he had probably done on many previous occasions. But this time her response was different: she replied, "I ain't no nigger. I's a Negro and I'm Miss Liza Mixon." Stung, the former master chased his former slave with a whip.[1]

Until the civil rights revolution of the 1960s, whites in the South typically refrained from addressing blacks as "Mr." or "Mrs." but instead called them by their first names or by titles signifying a senior with servile status—titles such as "Uncle" or "Auntie." Addressing all black men as "boys," regardless of their age, was another way for whites to observe Jim Crow etiquette.

Positive modifications to such practices have been effected

only through struggle. To avoid or at least minimize belittlement, some blacks made a habit of identifying themselves only by their last names. Blacks furiously objected to *Negro* being spelled with a lower- as opposed to an uppercase *N,* and on March 7, 1930, the editors of the *New York Times* announced that the paper would henceforth capitalize the *N* in *Negro.* The U.S. Government Printing Office followed suit three years later. Within a decade, capitalization would become the rule at the Supreme Court as well. [2]

Referring to blacks derogatorily as niggers, however, was the custom to which blacks objected most strongly. In 1939, when David O. Selznick was in the throes of producing *Gone With the Wind,* he received hundreds of letters from blacks warning him to remove all "nigger" references from his upcoming film. The letter writers were concerned because the novel on which the film was based was full of such references. So, too, were early drafts of the film script. Initially Selznick sought to solve the problem by promising that the N-word would not be spoken by any white characters, but once he had been made aware of the intensity of blacks' feelings, he resolved to prohibit its use entirely and took pains to publicize his decision. A form letter declared that his studio had been "in frequent communication with Mr. [Walter] White of the Society for the Advancement of Colored People, and has accepted his suggestions concerning the elimination of the word 'nigger' from our picture."[3]

In the years that followed, blacks began to win other, similar battles. By the 1940s, "sensitivities were sufficiently aroused for Joseph Conrad's *The Nigger of the Narcissus* (1897) to be removed from open shelves in school libraries; for Mar-jorie Kinnan Rawlings's *The Yearling* (1938) to be released in a 'school edition' that omitted two passages containing the word [*nigger*]; and for Agatha Christie's play *Ten Little Niggers* (1939) to be retitled for American consumption as *Ten Little Indians* (and then retitled again as *And Then There Were None)*."[4]

In the 1960s and the decades thereafter, campaigns against racial indecency gained unprecedented support in mounting countless challenges to racist cultural artifacts. Scores of land-marks on official maps, for example, once bore such names as Nigger Lake, Niggerhead Hill, and Old Nigger Creek. *Nigger,* as we have seen, can have many meanings. But in the context of naming landmarks—an endeavor monopolized until recently by white men—it is clear that the *nigger* memorial-ized on maps was not the *nigger* of irony or affection but the *nigger* of insult and contempt. Widespread anger at carto-graphic slurs prompted Secretary of the Interior Stewart Udall to insist in 1963 that the Board on Geographic Names replace all references to *Nigger* with *Negro*.[5]

That same year, during court proceedings in Etowah County, Alabama, a prosecutor insisted upon addressing white witnesses by their last names and black witnesses by their first. At issue in the proceedings was the legality of arrests of civil rights protesters. The prosecutor began his cross-examination of one of the protesters by asking her name. She replied, "Miss Mary Hamilton." Addressing her as "Mary," he asked who had arrested her. She repeated her full name and added, "Please address me correctly." The prosecutor nevertheless continued to call her simply Mary, and the judge directed her to answer the question. She refused, whereupon the judge held her in contempt of court and immediately imposed a jail sentence and a fine. His ruling, however, would not stand; the Supreme Court of the United States would later reverse it.[6]

In Mississippi in 1964, during a *successful* gubernatorial campaign, Paul Johnson repeatedly joked that the acronym NAACP stood for "Niggers, Apes, Alligators, Coons, and Possums."[7] Such an electoral outcome would be inconceivable today in any state. No serious politician, not even a David Duke, could casually and unapologetically refer to "niggers" and hope to win an election. *Nigger* has been belatedly but effectively stigmatized—an important, positive development in American culture.

Progress, however, begets new problems, and our subject is no exception. The very conditions that have helped to stigmatize *nigger* have also been conducive to the emergence of certain troubling tendencies. Among these latter are unjustified deception, overeagerness to detect insult, the repression of *good* uses of *nigger*, and the overly harsh punishment of those who use the N-word imprudently or even wrongly.

The stigmatization of *nigger* has unavoidably created an atmosphere in which people may be tempted to make false charges in order to exploit feelings of sympathy, guilt, and anger. The most notorious instance of such deception involved an allegation made by a black teenager named Tawana Brawley, who claimed that several white men had abducted her, raped her, and scrawled *nigger* on her body with feces. Her charges have now been fully discredited, though some still profess to believe her story.[8] Brawley, however, was not alone in seeking to exploit goodwill through a hoax. In 1995 Tisha Anderson, a black woman, and William Lee, her white boyfriend, insisted that they had received hateful messages ("Niggers don't belong here") and been victimized by vandals who had scrawled racist slurs on the walls and steps of their apartment building ("Niggers live here"). It was all a lie: *they* were the ones who had defaced the building, in an attempt to escape their lease.[9] In another case, Persey Harris III filed charges against the owner of a restaurant, asserting that the man had come after him with a stick while shouting racial epithets. Harris later confessed that he had lied and explained that he had been trying to create the predicate for a civil lawsuit.[10] A Maryland woman, Sonia James, charged that thugs had flooded her home, slashed her furniture, and spray-painted racial slurs on her walls. Insurance companies covered her claims, the police set up a station near her house, and many people, after hearing of the alleged hate crime, sent gifts of money, food, and clothes. In actuality, the vandal was James herself.[11]

In yet another case, Sabrina Collins, a black freshman at Emory University, claimed that someone had targeted her with death threats and racist graffiti. Her alleged ordeal became national news. At one point it was reported that she had been so traumatized by racist mistreatment that she had curled up into a fetal position and ceased speaking. Subsequently, however, it became clear that Collins herself had committed the acts in question. That a college student would perpetrate such a hoax was bad enough, but worse still was the reaction voiced by Otis Smith, the president of the Atlanta branch of the NAACP, who dismissed as largely irrelevant the finding that Collins had lied. Echoing Tawana Brawley's apologists, he maintained that to him, it did not matter "whether [Collins] did it or not."[12] Rather, what concerned Smith was "all the pressure these black students are under at these predominantly white schools."[13] If the hoax served to highlight that issue, he suggested, then he had no problem with Collins's means of publicity. It is difficult to imagine anything that could be more discrediting to a civic leader than the remarks attributed to Smith. Not only do they exhibit an egregious indifference to truthfulness in public discussion; they also indicate an inability to distinguish between a coherent political strategy and a pathetic escapade that was probably nothing more than a desperate plea for help.

Of all the things that have hurt the campaign against *nigger*-as-insult, unjustifiable lying and silly defenses have inflicted the most damage. But worrisome, too, are the badly mistaken attacks undertaken against people who never should have been seen as enemies.

One infamous round of wrongheaded protest was directed against David Howard, the white director of a municipal agency in Washington, D.C. Howard unwittingly entered the fray when he told members of his staff that in light of budgetary constraints, he would have to be "niggardly" with the money at his disposal. Apparently believing that *niggardly* (which means miserly or stingy) was related to *nigger*, a couple of Howard's black subordinates began a whispering campaign that blossomed into a public outcry. Howard resigned. The mayor of Washington, Anthony Williams, immediately accepted his resignation, declaring that Howard had shown poor judgment.

For several days afterward this incident became a focus of discussion in forums high and low. Some observers voiced indignation at Howard's language and refused to be mollified by explanations of the etymological difference between *nigger* and *niggardly*. "Do you really think," asked one Washingtonian, "[that Howard] didn't notice he had to pass 'nigger' before he could get to the 'dly'?"[14] In print, too, a few commentators maintained that Howard had shown poor judgment, a lapse for which he could justly be sanctioned. Julianne Malveaux, for example, wrote, "I have a bunch of dictionaries and I understand that 'niggardly' and 'niggling' are not the same as the N-word. But I am still annoyed, amazed, outdone [by Howard]. . . . He understands that perhaps there are other ways to indicate a tightness in a budget—that one might say 'parsimonious,' 'frugal,' or 'miserly.' No matter how many times teutonics attempts to trump ebonics, the fact is that the n-words—be it the N-word or 'niggardly'—rankle."[15] Others declined to attack Howard but suggested that *niggardly* and other, similar words prone to be misunderstood might be best avoided.[16] "Would the openly gay Howard not flinch, not even a little bit," columnist Debra Dickerson asked, "if a superior found a reason to mention tossing a 'faggot' on the fire or going outside to smoke a 'fag'? Two more perfectly harmless and obscure words—but why go there?"[17] Refusing to be bound by the dictionary definition of *niggardly*, Courtland Milloy of the *Washington Post* asserted that "when the subject of race is at hand . . . the only dictionary that counts is the one that gives meaning to human experience." Milloy placed a question mark over "any white person who says 'niggardly' . . . when [that person] could have said miserly."[18]

Many other commentators, however, took the opposite view, and sharply criticized the way Howard had been treated. Julian Bond, the chairman of the board of directors of the NAACP, remarked facetiously that "the Mayor has been niggardly in his judgment on this issue."[19] Writing in the Raleigh, North Carolina, *News and Observer,* Barry Saunders averred that the episode demonstrated the malevolent influence of "people whose antennae are always up, seeking out an affront where none exists so they can respond out of all proportion."[20] Similarly dismissive was the columnist Tony Snow, who pronounced Howard the victim of a "linguistic lynching." According to Snow, "David Howard got fired because some people in public employ were morons who a) didn't know the meaning of 'niggardly,' b) didn't know how to use a dictionary to discover the word's meaning and c) actually demanded that he apologize for their ignorance."[21]

Eventually Mayor Williams, who has been criticized as insufficiently "black" by many Washingtonians, offered Howard another position in the D.C. government and admitted that he had been wrong to accept his resignation without first educating himself fully about what had transpired. By then, though, the damage had been done. By fearfully deferring to excessive and uninformed outrage, the mayor had lowered his own standing in public opinion.

What happened in Washington will forever shadow the history of *niggardly* and serve as a benchmark of hypersensitivity. Around the same time, however, an even more alarming incident involving *niggardly* occurred at the University of Wisconsin at Madison, where a professor used the word during a lecture in a class he was teaching on Chaucer. A black student who was upset by the similarity between *niggardly* and *nigger* approached the professor after class to express her concerns. He apparently thanked her for sharing her perceptions with him and proceeded to explain the origin of *niggardly* and hence its distance from the N-word. In the next session the professor once again referred to *niggardly* and then defined it for the class. Notwithstanding the clarification, the same black student who had previously spoken with the professor stormed out of the classroom, crying. According to one news report, she referred to her experience in the Chaucer class as evidence of the need for a stringent speech code that would apply to all members of the faculty, regardless of the intent behind their "offensive" words.[22]

A misplaced protest notable for the distinguished character of its antagonists erupted in the pages of *Boston Magazine* in May 1998, following the publication of a long, largely complimentary article by Cheryl Bentsen about Henry Louis Gates Jr., the chair of the Department of Afro-American Studies at Harvard University. Gates is a controversial figure about whom it is virtually impossible to write without getting involved in the disputes that surround his celebrity. In this instance, however, disputation arose not from Bentsen's profile itself but from the title given to it by the editors of the magazine. The cover of the April issue featured the phrase

"Head Negro in Charge," a softened version of a term well known in black circles: "Head Nigger in Charge," or HNIC. Scores of readers objected, including one who declared in an agitated letter to the editor:

> The title is EXTREMELY RACIST!!! As a black American, I am outraged and insulted. The term [HNIC] was used in the days of slavery when white foremen would designate a black person to oversee (that is to keep in check) other blacks. The title shows your ignorance and indifference to the black community. I vow NEVER to purchase or support your magazine in any way. I will also rally every single person I know to boycott your magazine.[23]

Another reader wrote:

> I am a subscriber . . . who is really offended by the headline of the Gates article. I can accept that you did not mean offense; but if members of the black community express dismay at the use of language, it is appropriate to say: I am sorry. . . . I will refrain from using such language in the future.[24]

Craig Unger, then the editor of *Boston Magazine,* responded to the controversy by asserting:

> The term HNIC is part of the vernacular of black writers and intellectuals. It denotes the phenomenon of

the white establishment selecting one African-American to speak for the race. It was in that context that we used HNIC, and there was clearly no intent to offend. On the contrary, we are proud of our story, and we want nothing to overshadow it. Our use of the expression, however, has obviously upset some people, and I sincerely regret that.[25]

Many critics of the "HNIC" title proceeded as if their offended sensibilities alone should settle the matter—as if their sense of outrage necessarily made the act they objected to a bad act warranting an apology. Repeatedly, people voiced anger at *Boston Magazine* without troubling to state what justified their anger. Natalie Anderson's letter to the editor, for example, charged that the title of the article was "EXTREMELY RACIST," but it neglected to explain what was so racist about it. True, "HNIC" has historically denoted a black person who is in command of a given situation only thanks to the backing of whites.[26] But clearly the editors of *Boston Magazine* were aware of that meaning and simply wished to add a provocative and ironic twist to a largely admiring profile of a prominent black figure by suggesting that despite massive changes in race relations, whites still retain the power to select who among blacks will be accorded the mantle of leadership—a point that has been made by numerous black intellectuals, including Gates himself.

In truth, the anger directed at *Boston Magazine* had to do not so much with the content of the disparaged title as with its provenance—that is, the fact that the phrase had been co-opted by the magazine's white editors. For many people, *nig-ger* and its cognates take on completely different complexions depending on the speaker's race. Had the "HNIC" profile and title appeared in *Essence, Emerge, Ebony,* or some other black-owned publication, there would have been no controversy. But *Boston Magazine* is white-owned and marketed mainly to whites, situating "HNIC" in a context that, for some observers, raised several difficulties: the embarrassment of discussing certain racial topics before a predominantly white audience; fear of, and anger about, a white entrepreneur intruding into black cultural territory; and the suspicion that whatever the setting, whites derive racist pleasure out of hearing, saying, or even alluding to "nigger." For these reasons, even blacks who use *nigger* themselves adamantly insist that it is wrong for whites to do so.[27] On the album containing his "I hate niggers" skit, for example, Chris Rock also presents a sketch in which a white man approaches him after a performance and appreciatively repeats some of what Rock has just said onstage. The next sound heard is that of the white man being punched.[28] Rock's message is clear: white people cannot rightly say about blacks some of the things that blacks themselves say about blacks. Just as a son is privileged to address his mother in ways that outsiders cannot (at least not in the son's presence), so, too, is a member of a race privileged to address his racial kin in ways proscribed to others.

Although many whites follow this convention, some rebel. Two noteworthy examples are Carl Van Vechten and Quentin Tarantino.

Van Vechten sparked controversy when, in 1926, he published *Nigger Heaven,* a novel about black life in Harlem. The title alone alienated many blacks, including some who knew the author personally. Van Vechten had, for example, selected some lines of poetry by his friend Countee Cullen to serve as the epigraph for his book, but when he told the poet about his proposed title, he turned, in Van Vechten's words, "white with rage."[29] And soon their friendship ended. At an antilynching rally in Harlem, a protester burned a copy of *Nigger Heaven.* And in Boston, the book was banned.

Van Vechten was well aware that the title would singe the sensibilities of many potential readers. Even his own father objected to it: "Your 'Nigger Heaven' is a title I don't like," Charles Duane Van Vechten informed his son in 1925. "I have myself never spoken of a colored man as a 'nigger.' If you are trying to help the race, as I am assured you are, I think every word you write should be a respectful one towards the blacks."[30] Yet the younger Van Vechten persisted, emblazoning upon his novel a title that still sparks resentment.

It should not be overlooked, however, that while many blacks condemned *Nigger Heaven,* others—including some of the most admired black intellectuals of the day— applauded it. Charles Chesnutt, the first black professional man of letters, praised Van Vechten in a letter, telling him that he hoped that the novel would "have the success which its brilliancy and obvious honesty deserve." Walter White, himself a novelist as well as a leading official with the NAACP, expressed both admiration and regret that he had not thought of the title first. Paul Robeson sent Van Vechten a congratulatory telegram that stated, in part, "NIGGER HEAVEN AMAZ-

ING IN ITS ABSOLUTE UNDERSTANDING AND DEEP SYMPA-
THY THANKS FOR SUCH A BOOK." Charles S. Johnson, editor
of *Opportunity*, one of the key journals of the Harlem Renaissance, commented that he "wish[ed] a Negro had written it."
Along the same lines, novelist Nella Larsen mused, "Why, oh,
why, couldn't we have done something as big as this for ourselves?"[31]

James Weldon Johnson, author of "Lift Evr'y Voice and
Sing" (the "Negro National Anthem"), wrote an effusive
review in which he declared that Van Vechten had paid colored
people "the rare tribute of writing about them as people
rather than as puppets."[32] Later, in his autobiography, Johnson
would assert that "most of the Negroes who condemned *Nigger Heaven* did not read it; they were estopped by the title."
Looking toward the future, he would conjecture that "as the
race progresses it will become less and less susceptible to
hurts from such causes."[33] On this point he was clearly wrong,
for as we have seen, even in this new century *nigger* retains its
capacity to anger, inflame, and distract.

The white film director Quentin Tarantino has recently updated the racial politics triggered by Van Vechten's
novel by writing film scripts in which *nigger* figures prominently. Tarantino's leading man in *Jackie Brown,* a black gun
runner, casually uses the word throughout the film; in one
sequence he hugs a black underling and, with apparent affection, calls him "my nigger," only to murder him in cold blood a
few minutes later. In *True Romance,* Tarantino orchestrates a
confrontation between a white man and a Sicilian mobster.
The man knows that the mobster is about to kill him, and in a

final gesture of defiance, he laughingly tells him that since North African moors—"niggers"—conquered Sicily and had sex with Sicilian women, his ancestors must have been niggers. Further, the condemned man speculates that the Sicilian's grandmother "fucked a nigger" and that therefore the mobster himself is "part eggplant." And in Tarantino's *Pulp Fiction,* a scene featuring a black hit man, his white partner, and a white friend of the black hit man has the professional assassins showing up unexpectedly at the home of the friend to dispose of a bloody car with a corpse inside. Exasperated, the white friend complains to his black hit-man buddy that "storing dead niggers ain't my fucking business." It isn't so much the fact that he will be breaking the law by helping to conceal a murder that worries him; rather, it's the fear that his wife will divorce him if she comes home while the hit men are still in the house. This white man who talks of "dead-nigger storage" loves his wife and is absolutely terrified by the prospect of losing her. It is important to note that she is black.

Spike Lee, among others, has taken exception to Tarantino's playfulness with *nigger*. When it was noted in response that some of his own films also make extensive use of *nigger,* the director replied that as an African American, he had "more of a right to use [the N-word]."[34] Lee himself has not articulated the basis for that asserted "right," but at least three theories are plausible. One is that the long and ugly history of white racist subordination of African Americans should in and of itself disqualify whites from using *nigger*. A second holds that equity earned through oppression grants cultural ownership rights: having been made to suffer by being called "nigger" all these years, this theory goes, blacks should now be able to monopolize the slur's peculiar cultural capital.[35] A third theory is that whites lack a sufficiently intimate knowledge of black culture to use the word *nigger* properly.

All three of these theories are dramatized in Lee's film *Bamboozled,* a farce about a black scriptwriter who, in order to keep his job, creates a television-network variety show featuring all of the stereotypical characteristics through which blacks have been comically defamed: blackface, bugging eyes, extravagant buffoonery, the omnipresent grin. Lee takes care to make the worst of *Bamboozled*'s many villains an obnoxious, presumptuous, ignorant white man—Dunwitty—who deems himself sufficiently "black" to boast to his African American subordinates that he knows more about "niggers" than they do.[36]

The great failing of these theories is that, taken seriously, they would cast a protectionist pall over popular culture that would likely benefit certain minority entrepreneurs only at the net expense of society overall. Excellence in culture thrives, like excellence elsewhere, in a setting open to competition—and that includes competition concerning how best to dramatize the N-word. Thus, instead of cordoning off racially defined areas of the culture and allowing them to be tilled only by persons of the "right" race, we should work toward enlarging the common ground of American culture, a field that is open to all comers regardless of their origin. Despite Spike Lee's protests to the contrary, Quentin Tarantino is talented and has the goods to prove it. That is not to say that he should be exempt from criticism, but Lee's racial critique of his fellow director is off the mark. It is almost wholly ad hominem. It focuses on the character of Tarantino's race rather than the character of his work—brilliant work that allows the word *nigger* to be heard in a rich panoply of contexts and intonations.

In 1997 in Ypsilanti, Michigan, a computer technician named Delphine Abraham decided to look up the definition of *nigger* in the tenth edition of *Merriam-Webster's Collegiate Dictionary*.[37] This is what she found:

> **1:** a black person—usu. taken to be offensive **2:** a member of any dark-skinned race—usu. taken to be offensive **3:** a member of a socially disadvantaged class of persons <it's time for somebody to lead all of America's ~s . . . all the people who feel left out of the political process—Ron Dellums>
>
> ***usage*** *Nigger* in senses 1 and 2 can be found in the works of such writers of the past as Joseph Conrad, Mark Twain, and Charles Dickens, but it now ranks as perhaps the most offensive and inflammatory racial slur in English. Its use by and among blacks is not always intended or taken as offensive, but, except in sense 3, it is otherwise a word expressive of racial hatred and bigotry.

Abraham recorded what she subsequently felt and did:

I felt that the first two definitions labeled me and any-one else who happened to be Black or have dark skin a nigger. Outraged, I called Merriam-Webster in Spring-field, Massachusetts. I reached the company's president and publisher, John Morse, who was polite but really didn't seem to understand my concerns. Not getting a response that satisfied me, I told him before hanging up, "Something should be done about this, and I think I'm going to start a petition drive to have the word removed or redefined."

Just by speaking locally, I gathered more than 2,000 signatures within the first month. I was interviewed by the Associated Press news service, on radio talk shows, and even on CNN. Newsgroups on the Internet joined the campaign. Syndicated newspaper columnists weighed in. The NAACP, through its president and CEO, Kweisi Mfume, suggested organizing a boycott if Merriam-Webster did not review the definition.

Most people believe, as I do, that the N-word needs a more accurate first definition reflecting that it is a derogatory term used to dehumanize or oppress a group or race of people.[38]

The question is, should Abrahams, Mfume, or anyone else have felt insulted by Merriam-Webster's definition?

No.

The definition notes that the term is usually taken to be offensive and then states, for good measure, that the N-word "now ranks as perhaps the most offensive and inflammatory racial slur in English." Abrahams claimed that the Merriam-Webster definition labeled as a nigger anyone who happened to be black. But that view is unreasonable given the totality of the definition offered by the dictionary. In defining *nigger,* moreover, Webster's 10th does not vary from its typical practice. For instance, in defining *honky,* the dictionary posits: "*usu. disparaging:* a white person."

In response to Abraham's petition drive, representatives of Merriam-Webster tried to depoliticize the matter by portraying the dictionary as a mechanical, autonomous linguistic mirror. To this end, the marketing director repeatedly averred that "a dictionary is a scholarly reference, not a political tool. As long as the word is in use, it is our responsibility as dictionary publishers to put the word into the dictionary."[39] Similarly, the company president, John R. Morse, portrayed his editors as mere technicians lacking independent powers of their own. Dictionary makers, Morse maintained, "do not invent the words that go into the dictionary, and they don't decide what meanings they will have."[40] Morse simultaneously undermined his own point, however, by noting that "offensive words . . . appear only in hardcover college-level dictionaries, which are edited expressly for adults. Slurs and other offensive words are not included in dictionaries intended for children. Nor are they published in any smaller, abridged dictionaries, such as paperbacks." With respect to these other dictionaries, the managers of Merriam-Webster had decided, for various reasons, to excise the N-word. Whether or not this decision was a sound one is, for the moment, irrelevant. The important thing to recognize is that dictionary makers do, in fact, exercise judgment, notwithstanding Morse's evasive denial.

Deciding whether to note or how to define a deeply controversial word is an inescapably "political" act, and claims to the contrary are either naive or disingenuous. The issue, then, is not whether editors shape the substance of their dictionaries. Of course they do. The issue is the substance of the choices made. Some of Merriam-Webster's critics have condemned the editors' decision to include any reference at all to *nigger*. "If the word is not there [in the dictionary], you can't use it," one protester asserted in favor of deleting the N-word altogether.[41] That tack, however, is glaringly wrongheaded. Many terms that are absent from dictionaries are nonetheless pervasive in popular usage. Moreover, so long as racist sentiments exist, they will find linguistic means of expression, even if some avenues are blocked. There are, after all, numerous ways of insulting people.

In sum, the campaign against *Merriam-Webster's Collegiate Dictionary* was misguided. The dictionary defined the term adequately, and the dictionary's editors were correct in including the N-word despite the embarrassment and hurt feelings the term inflicts. *Nigger* should have a place in any serious dictionary. The word is simply too important to ignore.

A second, and achingly poignant, example of mistaken protest is the widespread repudiation of *Huckleberry Finn*, now one of the most beleaguered texts in American literature. Monthly, it seems, someone attacks Mark Twain's most famous book on the grounds that it is racist. The novel's most energetic foe, John H. Wallace, calls it "the most grotesque example of racist trash ever written."[42] For many of *Huckleberry Finn*'s enemies, the most upsetting and best proof of the book's racism is the fact that *nigger* appears in the text some 215 times. At one point, for example, Huck's aunt Sally asks him why he is so late arriving at her house:

> "We blowed a cylinder head."
> "Good gracious! Anybody hurt?"
> "No'm. Killed a nigger."
> "Well, it's lucky; because sometimes people do get hurt."[43]

Wallace asserts that this exchange, within the context of the novel as a whole, strives to make the point that blacks are not human beings.[44] That interpretation, however, is ludicrous, a frightening exhibition of how thought becomes stunted in the absence of any sense of irony. Twain is not willfully buttressing racism here; he is seeking ruthlessly to unveil and ridicule it. By putting *nigger* in white characters' mouths, the author is not branding blacks, but rather branding the whites.

There was a time when Twain's own use of *nigger* signaled contempt. As a young man inculcated with white-supremacist beliefs and sentiments, he viewed blacks as inferior and spoke of them as such.[45] As he matured and traveled and became more cosmopolitan, however, Twain underwent a dramatic metamorphosis. He grew to hate slavery and the brutality of Jim Crow and began to express his antiracist perspective satirically through his writings. *Huckleberry Finn* is the best fictive example of Twain's triumph over his upbringing. In it he creates a loving relationship between Huck and Jim, the runaway slave, all the while sardonically impugning the pretensions of white racial superiority. Among Twain's nonfiction, a striking example of his revolt against bigotry is his piece "Only a Nigger," in which he speaks in the voice of an apologist for a lynching:

> Ah, well! Too bad, to be sure! A little blunder in the administration of justice by southern mob-law: but nothing to speak of. Only "a nigger" killed by mistake—that is all. . . . But mistakes will happen, even in the conduct of the best regulated and most high-toned mobs, and surely there is no good reason why Southern gentlemen should worry themselves with useless regrets, so long as only an innocent "nigger" is hanged, or roasted or [ ] to death now and then. . . . What are the lives of a few "niggers" in comparison with the impetuous instincts of a proud and fiery race? Keep ready the halter, therefore, o chivalry of Memphis! Keep the lash knotted; keep the brand and the faggots in waiting, for prompt work with the next "nigger" who may be suspected of any damnable crime![46]

Wallace, I suppose, would read this as an endorsement of lynching. But obviously it is intended to be just the opposite. The same holds true for *Huckleberry Finn*, which Twain designed to subvert, not to reinforce, racism.

I am not ruling out criticism of the novel. Perceptive com-

mentators have questioned its literary merits.[47] It is undoubtedly true, moreover, that regardless of Twain's intentions,
Huckleberry Finn (like *any* work of art) can be handled in a way
that is not only stupid but downright destructive of the educational and emotional well-being of students. To take a contemporary example, the producers of *Mississippi Burning* intended
their film to carry an antiracist message, but that did not prevent it from contributing inspiration to a wayward youth who,
in 1990, burned crosses outside the residence of a black family
in St. Paul, Minnesota, in an effort to frighten them into
moving.[48]

Such concerns, however, are different from the one I am
addressing. I am addressing the contention that the presence of
nigger alone is sufficient to taint *Huckleberry Finn* or any other
text. I am addressing those who contend that *nigger* has *no*
proper place in American culture and who thus desire to erase
the N-word totally, without qualification, from the cultural
landscape. I am addressing parents who, in numerous locales,
have demanded the removal of *Huckleberry Finn* from syllabi
solely on the basis of the presence of the N-word—without
having read the novel themselves, without having investigated
the way in which it is being explored in class, and without considering the possibilities opened up by the close study of a text
that confronts so dramatically the ugliness of slavery and
racism. I am addressing eradicationists who, on grounds of
racial indecency, would presumably want to bowdlerize or
censor poems such as Carl Sandburg's "Nigger Lover," stories
such as Theodore Dreiser's "Nigger Jeff," Claude McKay's
"Nigger Lover," or Henry Dumas' "Double Nigger," plays such

as Ed Bullins' *The Electronic Nigger,* and novels such as Gil Scott-Heron's *The Nigger Factory.*

A third category of misguided protest involves cases in which insulted parties demand excessive punishment. Consider what happened in 1993 at Central Michigan University (CMU).

Keith Dambrot was in his third year as the school's varsity men's basketball coach.[49] CMU also designated him as an "assistant professor"; presumably his subject was basketball. At halftime during a game against Miami University of Ohio, Dambrot tried to focus and inspire his team, made up of eleven blacks and three whites. He asked his players for permission to use with them a term that they often used with one another: the N-word. They nodded their assent, at which point Coach Dambrot said, "We need to be tougher, harder-nosed, and play harder. . . . We need to have more niggers on the team."[50] He then admiringly referred to one white member of the team as a nigger and went around the locker room categorizing the other players, by name, as either niggers or half-niggers. The niggers were the players who were doing their jobs well. The half-niggers or non-niggers were the ones who needed to work harder. Coach Dambrot later explained that he had used the term *nigger* "for instructional purposes with the permission of my African American players, and I used the term in the sense in which it is used by my African American players . . . to connote a person who is fearless, mentally strong, and tough."[51]

Despite the halftime pep talk, Central Michigan lost the

game. But that was merely the beginning of Coach Dambrot's problems.

Word soon spread on campus about Coach Dambrot's locker-room speech. He must have become aware of this, and realized that some observers might take offense, because he asked the university's athletic director to speak to the members of the team about the incident. None of them voiced any objection to what the coach had said. Nonetheless, the athletic director told Dambrot that regardless of his intentions, his use of *nigger* had been "extremely inappropriate."[52] The director then warned the coach that if he used the term again, he would be fired.

Soon thereafter, a student who had previously quit the basketball team complained about the coach's language to the university's affirmative-action officer. This administrator, a white woman, demanded that the coach be punished. She insisted that a formal reprimand be placed in his personnel file, that he be suspended without pay for five days, and that during his suspension he arrange for a sensitivity trainer to meet with the team to explain why the use of *nigger* was always inappropriate. She further specified that attendance at this sensitivity-training session should be made mandatory, that Coach Dambrot should "help assure that the team is not hostile to the training," and that he should "convey his support of this training session to the players and the staff."[53]

The coach did not resist, hoping that the incident would blow over quietly. His hopes, however, were shortly to be dashed. Publicity triggered two demonstrations at which eighty to a hundred protesters expressed their disapproval of the coach's purported "racism." The president of the university responded by announcing that the coach had been disciplined, declaring that "the term [*nigger*] is inappropriate under any circumstances," and avowing that he was "deeply sorry about the hurt, anger, [and] embarrassment its use ha[d] caused individuals as well as the entire university community."[54] By that time, though, critics of the university, including state legislators, were calling for harsher punishment, which was soon forthcoming.

On April 12, 1993, the university administration fired Coach Dambrot on the grounds that "public reaction to the incident [had] created an environment that makes it impossible for the university to conduct a viable basketball program under [his] leadership."[55]

Dambrot then sued the university, claiming that his discharge constituted a violation of his First Amendment rights. In a gesture of solidarity, members of the basketball team also sued the university, claiming that its speech code violated *their* First Amendment rights. The students prevailed—judges invalidated CMU's speech code—but not so their coach: judges ruled that the First Amendment did not bar the university from firing him. As interpreted by the Supreme Court, the First Amendment protects (to some extent) speech that touches upon matters of public concern. Therefore, if the coach had been talking to his team at halftime about, say, the racist history of the term *nigger*, his comments probably would have been protected. But in the view of the judges, Dambrot's speech did not touch upon a matter of public concern and was therefore fully vulnerable to the university's censure.

Here, however, I am interested not so much in the courts' conclusion that the university had the authority to fire the coach—a legal conclusion that seems to me to have been correct—as in the judgment that the university officials exercised pursuant to that authority. That judgment—or, more accurately, that *mis*judgment—casts a revealing light on our society's continued grappling with *nigger* and the cultural dynamics that surround it. The initial response by the athletic director—ordering the coach to desist—was sufficient. It recognized the undue risk that the coach's words might be misunderstood by members of the wider university community, while acknowledging that Dambrot had meant no harm.

Subsequent actions taken by university officials were excessive. First, the sensitivity-training session ordered by the affirmative-action officer was just the sort of Orwellian overreaching that has, unfortunately, tarnished the reputation of multiculturalist reformism. Among her requirements in regard to the session, after all, were that it must brook no debate over the propriety of the coach's language; that it must involve the coach in pacifying his players' resistance; that player attendance must be mandatory; and that the coach must explicitly state his support for the process regardless of his own opinions. Second, prior to firing Coach Dambrot, CMU officials seem to have made little effort to clarify the controversy or to suggest to the university community that this was a situation in which underlying realities were considerably more ambiguous than surface appearances might indicate. The fact is that Dambrot, though imprudent, was obviously employing *nigger* in a sense embraced by his players—a sense in which the term was a compliment, not an insult.[56] Sometimes it may be necessary for an administration to sacrifice a deserving employee in order to mollify public anger that might otherwise pose a threat to the institution's future. In this case, however, the CMU authorities capitulated too quickly to the formulaic rage of affronted blacks, the ill-considered sentimentality of well-meaning whites, and their own crass, bureaucratic opportunism.

An even more deplorable incident took place in 1998 at Jefferson Community College in Louisville, Kentucky, where an adjunct professor named Ken Hardy taught a course on interpersonal communications.[57] In a class exploring taboo words, students cited a number of insulting terms such as *faggot* and *bitch*. A member of the class mentioned *nigger*, and in the course of the discussion, Hardy repeated it. One of the nine black students in the twenty-two-person class objected to the airing of *that* word. Classmates disagreed, giving rise to a debate in which most of those present participated. At one point Hardy lent his support to the student who had first objected, suggesting that the class should take seriously the proposition that certain words were simply too volatile to be spoken out loud.

During a break, the student who had objected approached Hardy and requested that he stop using the N-word. Hardy defended the class discussion that had transpired but offered the student the option of sitting out the remainder of the session. She rejected that alternative. Subsequently she noted her continued disapproval in a letter to Hardy and also relayed her complaint to the Reverend Louis Coleman, a prominent local civil rights activist. Coleman, in turn, called the president of the college and asked him to "look into the matter." Hardy soon found himself in a tense meeting with the acting dean of academic affairs, who indicated, among other things, that the school could ill afford to antagonize prominent citizens. Although Hardy did not know it at the time, his career at Jefferson was at an end. A few days later the dean left a message on his phone stating that he would have no job at the college come fall.

The dismissal at Jefferson was worse than the one at CMU because it arose from a teacher's effort to make a point that was directly relevant to the intellectual concerns of a college-level course. By contrast, Coach Dambrot had acted imprudently in gratuitously using the word *nigger* in a context readily available to misinterpretation. Common to both cases, however, was the overeagerness of academic administrators to fire a subordinate for a *single* perceived misstep, even in circumstances in which the alleged wrongdoer had quite obviously been innocent of any intention to insult or otherwise harm those whom he addressed.

A much more sensible and humane response was modeled by high school students in Gould, Arkansas, in 1988.[58] A white teacher got into trouble because of a remark she made to an all-black class of students who were, according to her, becoming rambunctious. Exasperated, she said something designed to get their attention: "I think you're trying to make me think

you're a bunch of poor, dumb niggers, and I don't think that."
Upon hearing about her comment, ninety-one parents signed
a petition demanding her removal. The school board
requested the teacher's resignation after she acknowledged
that she had committed "a dumb, stupid mistake." She was
reportedly about to leave the town for good when students
circulated petitions asking the board to reconsider its decision. The petitions were signed by 124 out of the town's 147
high school students, only two of whom were white. In light of
this development, the school board, chaired by a black man,
reversed itself. Asked to explain the students' intervention, a
student leader replied, "We were ready to forgive and go
on. . . . Anybody ought to get a second chance."

The student's statement, generous as it is, needs a bit of
qualification. The offer of a second chance ought not to be
automatic but should instead hinge on such variables as the
nature of the offender's position and the purpose behind his or
her remark. In contrast to District Attorney Spivey, the
teacher held a position that, while important, did not entail
her exercising powers like those wielded by a prosecutor.
Moreover, again in contrast to District Attorney Spivey, the
teacher was not attempting to humiliate anyone. She was simply trying to instruct her students for their own benefit, albeit
in a regrettable manner. In such circumstances she, like Coach
Dambrot, deserved a second chance.

Advocates of broader prohibitions against "hate speech" maintain that the current legal regime is all too tolerant of *nigger*-
as-insult and other forms of racial abuse. Several of the most

prominent of these advocates—notably Charles Lawrence, Mari Matsuda, and Richard Delgado—have, in their positions as professors in law schools, provided intellectual underpinnings for campaigns aimed at banishing hate speech.[59] They and their allies have succeeded in persuading authorities at some colleges and universities to enact new speech codes. They have succeeded, too, in shaking up and enlivening civil libertarians, a group that had become intellectually complacent in the absence of a strong challenge. They have been unable, however, to sway the judiciary and have thus been forced to witness the invalidation of speech codes tested in litigation.[60] They have also largely failed to capture opinion. In the American culture wars of the 1980s and 1990s, the left-liberal multiculturalists who sought increased regulation of hate speech were soundly trounced by a coalition of opponents who effectively derided them as censorious ideologues—otherwise known as the P.C. (Political Correctness) Police.

The point, however, is not simply that the champions of speech codes lost on a variety of important fronts; it is that they *rightly* lost. For one thing, proponents of enhanced hate-speech regulation have typically failed to establish persuasively the asserted predicate for their campaign—that is, that verbal abuse on college campuses and elsewhere is a "rising," "burgeoning," "growing," "resurgent" development demanding countermeasures.[61] Regulationists do cite racist incidents on campus—the African student at Smith College who found a message slipped under her door reading, "African Nigger do you want some bananas?";[62] the counselor at Purdue University who was greeted by the words "Death Nigger" etched onto her door;[63] the taunt written on a blackboard at the University of Michigan: "A mind is a terrible thing to waste—especially on a nigger"[64]—but too often the dramatic retelling of an anecdote is permitted to substitute for a more systematic, quantitative analysis. Indeed, some commentators do not even seriously attempt to document their assertions but instead simply note a number of apparently outrageous events and then charge, without substantiation, that these episodes are, for example, representative of "a rise in the incidence of verbal and symbolic assault and harassment to which black and other traditionally subjugated groups are subjected."[65] A list of twenty, fifty, one hundred, or even three hundred racist incidents may appear to offer a terrible indictment of race relations on American campuses—until one recalls that there are hundreds of institutions of higher education across the country. Bearing in mind the numbers of young collegians who are constantly interacting with one another, often in close quarters, is a useful aid for keeping in perspective the catalogue of racist episodes that regulationists point to as the predicate for what they see as urgently needed reform.

A persuasive assertion that racially assaultive speech is on the rise ought logically to entail positing that there was a greater incidence of such speech in year Y than in year X. Demonstrating such a trajectory, however, is a daunting enterprise. After all, even when one is able to say that the number of reported incidents in a certain year was greater than the number of reported incidents in another year, there remains the problem of determining whether the reporting itself was a mirror of reality or a result of efforts to elicit from subjects their dissatisfaction with conduct they perceived to be offensive. Acknowledging such complications opens the way to considering alternative interpretations to those put forth by the regulationists. One alternative is that the growing number of reported episodes involving hate speech is a function of both an increased willingness to report perceived insults and an increased willingness to record them, which would mean that the perception of a rising tide of racial vilification is an illusion that paradoxically signals progress rather than regress. Or it may be that the regulationists are correct—that increased reporting does in fact reflect a greater incidence of verbal abuse. Even if that is so, however, there remains a question of interpretation. Here again, it is possible that episodes of verbal abuse are actually indicative of racial progress. On some campuses, for example, racist verbal abuse may not previously have been a problem simply because there were too few blacks around to generate racial friction. More recently, with the advent of a critical mass of black students, the possibilities for racial conflict may have escalated. At institutions where this is the case, increasing numbers of racial insults could be merely a function of more frequent interracial interaction and all that comes with it—for good and for ill.

Proponents of enhanced speech codes portray blacks on predominantly white campuses as being socially isolated and politically weak. Yet the regulationists clearly believe that the authorities to whom they are appealing are likely to side with these students and not with their antagonists. This, as Henry Louis Gates Jr. observes, is the "hidden foundation for the [anti–] hate speech movement. . . .You don't go to the teacher to complain about the school bully unless you know the teacher is on your side."[66]

Resorting to school authorities, however, has had its own costs. In stressing the "terror" of verbal abuse, proponents of hate-speech regulation have, ironically, empowered abusers while simultaneously weakening black students by counseling that they should feel grievously wounded by remarks that their predecessors would have shaken off or ignored altogether.

An examination of the substance of the regulationists' proposals turns up suggested reforms that are puzzlingly narrow, frighteningly broad, or disturbingly susceptible to discriminatory manipulation. In 1990, after much debate, Stanford University prohibited "harassment by personal vilification," which it defined as speech or other expression that

a) is intended to insult or stigmatize an individual or a small number of individuals on the basis of their race, color, handicap, religion, sexual orientation, or national and ethnic origin; and

b) is addressed directly to the individual or individuals whom it insults or stigmatizes; and

c) makes use of insulting or "fighting" words or nonverbal symbols.[67]

Perhaps the most notable feature of this provision is how little it accomplished. One of the incidents at Stanford that had fueled the call for a speech code in the first place involved the defacement of a poster bearing a likeness of Beethoven. After an argument with a black student who claimed that the composer had been partly of African descent, white students darkened a portrait of him and exaggerated the curliness of his hair and the thickness of his lips. They then affixed their negrofied poster to the door of the black student's room. Regulationists were outraged by this conduct, which they perceived as being aggressively racist. But the Stanford code would not have covered this action or, for that matter, most of the other verbal or symbolic "assaults" about which regulationists complain. During the first five years of Stanford's code, in fact, no one was ever charged with a violation. Some might argue that this record suggests that the code effectively prevented bad conduct, thus obviating the need for disciplinary proceedings. But a more plausible explanation is that conduct of the sort prohibited by the code was virtually nonexistent before its enactment and virtually nonexistent afterward—a veritable straw man.[68]

The Stanford code covered a single, specific type of speech: vulgar racial insults directed from one person to another in a face-to-face encounter. Such exchanges do happen; at the University of Wisconsin, for instance, a group of white male students reportedly followed some black female students, all the while shouting, "I've never tried a nigger before."[69] But conduct of this sort is sanctionable via traditional legal machinery (or if not through reputation-besmirching publicity), without resort to newfangled modes of repression. It is likely, moreover, that especially on a college campus, antiblack polemics that are polite, skillful, and conventionally garbed—think of *The Bell Curve*—will be far more hurtful to African Americans than the odd *nigger, coon, jigaboo,* or other racial insult, which in any case will almost certainly be more discrediting to the speaker than to the target. Yet under the Stanford code, the damaging but polite polemic is protected, while the rude but impotent epithet is not. This problem of underinclusiveness is a major embarrassment for the regulationist camp because, as Gates notes, "the real power commanded by the racist is likely to vary inversely with the vulgarity with which it is expressed. Black professionals soon learn that it is the socially disenfranchised—the lower class, the homeless—who are more likely to hail them as 'niggers.' The circles of power have long since switched to a vocabulary of indirection." By focusing on vulgar words that wound, regulationists "invite us to spend more time worr[ying] about speech codes than [about] coded speech."[70]

Because speech codes of the Stanford variety fail to address what some regulationists see as intolerable forms of speech, broader prohibitions have been proposed. Professor Charles Lawrence, for example, has urged that the ban on racial epithets be extended beyond the context of face-to-face encounters, while Professor Mari Matsuda has advocated punishing "racist speech" in general. Such proposals, however, encroach upon legal doctrines that have helped to make American culture among the most open and vibrant in the world.[71] Under the overbreadth doctrine, regulation must be narrowly drawn so as to touch only that conduct which a governing authority may validly repress; where a regulation sweeps within its ambit a substantial amount of protected speech along with unprotected conduct, the overbreadth doctrine instructs courts to invalidate the regulation. Under the vagueness doctrine, regulation that may chill protected expression must be drawn with especially rigorous exactitude. And under the doctrine of content neutrality, a governmental authority cannot prohibit certain forms of speech merely because it objects to the ideas or sentiments the speaker seeks to communicate. To quote one of many Supreme Court pronouncements on this theme: "If there is one star fixed in our constitutional constellation, it is that no official, high or petty, can prescribe what shall be orthodox in politics, nationalism, religion or other matters of opinion."[72] The cumulative effect of these and related speech-protective doctrines is a conspicuous toleration of speech and other representations that many people—in some instances the vast majority of people—find deeply, perhaps even viscerally, obnoxious, including flag burning, pornography, Nazis' taunting of Holocaust survivors, a jacket emblazoned with the phrase "Fuck the Draft" worn in a courthouse, *The Satanic Verses*, *The Birth of a Nation*, *The Last Temptation of Christ*. And just as acute wariness of public or private censorship has long furthered struggles for freedom of expression in all its many guises, so has resistance against censorship always been an important and positive feature of the great struggles against racist tyranny in the United States, from the fight against slavery to the fight against Jim Crow.[73] For this reason, we may count ourselves fortunate that the anti–hate-speech campaign of the regulationists fizzled and has largely subsided. This particular effort to do away with *nigger*-as-insult and its kindred symbols was simply not worth the various costs that success would have exacted.

———

Finally, I turn to the eradicationists—those who maintain that *all* uses of *nigger* are wrongful and hurtful and ought to be condemned by dint of public opinion. Their absolutist position simply fails to acknowledge adequately either the malleability of language or the complexity of African American communities. Even the proponents of enhanced speech codes—the "regulationists" whom I have just criticized—make a distinction between racist and nonracist, impermissible and permissible usages of the N-word. Professor Delgado has proposed, for example, that whites who insultingly call blacks niggers should be subject to suit for money damages. He goes on to explain, however, that the salutation " 'Hey, nigger,' spoken affectionately between black persons and used as a greeting, would not be actionable" under his scheme.[74] Similarly, though without expressly mentioning *nigger,* Professor Matsuda has indicated that her approach would allow words generally seen as racial insults, and thus otherwise prohibitable, to be protected in the context of a "particular subordinated community" that tolerated the use of such terms as a form of "wordplay."[75] She elaborates, "Where this is the case, community members tend to have a clear sense of what is racially degrading and what is not. The appropriate standard in determining whether language is persecutorial, hateful, and degrading is the recipient's community standard. We should avoid further victimization of subordinated groups by misunderstanding their linguistic and cultural norms."[76]

Matsuda, however, minimizes the reality of cultural conflict within groups. As we have seen, for example, blacks differ sharply over the use of *nigger*. Some condemn it absolutely, unequivocally, across the board, no matter who is voicing the hated N-word and no matter what the setting. This has long been so. Writing in 1940, Langston Hughes remarked:

> The word *nigger* to colored people of high and low degree is like a red rag to a bull. Used rightly or wrongly, ironically or seriously, of necessity for the sake of realism, or impishly for the sake of comedy[,] it doesn't matter. Negroes do not like it in any book or play whatsoever, be the book or play ever so sympathetic in its treatment of the basic problems of the race. The word *nigger*, you see, sums up for us who are colored all the bitter years of insult and struggle in America.[77]

Hughes overgeneralized. *All* Negroes do not react to *nigger* in the way he described. Hughes himself did not; he applauded his friend Carl Van Vechten's novel *Nigger Heaven*. He was also certainly aware that blacks used "nigger" freely when outside the presence of whites.[78] Hughes was correct, though, in suggesting that some blacks—then as now—detest *nigger* so thoroughly that they eschew efforts to distinguish between good and bad usages of the term and instead condemn it out of hand. "Everyone should refrain from [using the N-word] and provide negative sanctions on its use by others," black-studies professor Halford H. Fairchild has argued. What about blacks' using the term ironically, as a term of affection? "The persistent viability of the N-word in the black community," Fairchild writes, "is a scar from centuries of cultural racism."[79] Voicing the same message, Ron Nelson, an editor of the University of North Carolina newspaper, notes that while "most blacks . . . understand the implications and racist history of the word *nigger,* it has somehow dangerously and disturbingly found its way into everyday language." Castigating blacks' playful use of the N-word as "self-defeating," "hypocritical," and "absurd," Nelson asserts that its usage "creates an atmosphere of acceptance [in which whites wonder,] After all, if blacks themselves do it, why can't others[?]"[80] The Pulitzer Prize–winning journalist E. R. Shipp is of the same opinion. In an article revealingly entitled "N-Word Just as Vile When Uttered by Blacks," Shipp declared that "there needs to be no confusion. . . . The N-word has no place in contemporary life or language."[81]

Bill Cosby is another who attacks blacks' use of *nigger.* Addressing African American comedians, Cosby has argued that when *nigger* pops out of their mouths as entertainment, all blacks are hurt. He fears that white onlookers will have negative impressions of African Americans reinforced when blacks laughingly bandy about the N-word. He fears that many whites largely ignorant of black America will be all too literal-minded and will fail to understand the joke. Notwithstanding Cosby's criticisms and pleas, many black comedians have continued to give *nigger* a prominent place in their acts. Several of them were mainstays of *Def Comedy Jam,* a popular show that appeared on the Home Box Office cable-television network in the 1990s. Taking aim at *Def Comedy Jam,* Cosby likened it to an updated *Amos 'n' Andy:* "When you watch [*Def Comedy Jam*], you hear a statement or a joke and it says 'niggers.' And sometimes they say 'we niggers.' And we are laughing [at it], just as we laughed at *Amos 'n' Andy* in the fifties. But we don't realize that there are people watching who know nothing about us. This is the only picture they have of us other than our mothers going to work in their homes and pushing their children in the carriages and dusting their houses. . . . And they say, 'Yeah, that's them. Just like we thought.' "[82]

Cosby's reference to *Amos 'n' Andy* was intended to damn *Def Comedy Jam* by associating it with a program that some blacks regard as a terrible affront to African Americans.[83] *Amos 'n' Andy* began as a radio show in 1928. It was written and dramatized by two white men with roots in minstrelsy who animated the misadventures of a group of blacks living and working in Harlem. Episodes of the show focused on marital woes and infidelities, inept efforts to realize professional or entrepreneurial ambitions, and petty bickering within a semi-secret fraternal order named the Mystic Knights of the Sea. Among the show's personalities were Andy (an amiable dunce), the Kingfish (a schemer who constantly bilked stupid Andy), Amos (an earnest taxicab driver), Algonquin J. Calhoun (an inept and unethical attorney), Sapphire (Andy's angry, contemptuous, shrewish wife), and Lightnin' (a slow, easily befuddled housepainter).

Amos 'n' Andy was one of the most successful programs in the history of radio. It inspired a comic strip, a candy bar, greeting cards, phonograph records, and a film. It coined phrases—for example, "holy mackerel"—that have become embedded in colloquial speech, and touched hundreds of thousands of Americans in all manner of surprising ways. Owners of restaurants, hotels, and movie theaters piped the show into their establishments for fear that if they didn't, customers would leave in droves to hear the latest installment. Eleanor Roosevelt was a fan, as was Huey P. Long, the flamboyant, demagogic governor of Louisiana, who nicknamed himself Kingfish under the show's influence.

In 1951, when *Amos 'n' Andy* moved to television, an all-black cast (the first on network TV) superseded the white men who had previously supplied the voices of the black characters. Although the show lasted only two seasons, syndicated reruns would be aired on local television stations until the mid-1960s.

Amos 'n' Andy's harshest critics denounced it as "the ultimate metaphor of whites' casual contempt for blacks."[84] W. J. Walls, a bishop in the African Methodist Episcopal Zion Church, contended in 1929 that the radio program degraded blacks by presenting African American characters with "crude, repetitional, moronic mannerisms" who spoke "gibbberish." Bishop Walls stated that there did exist "unlettered and mentally imbecilic" Negroes. But *Amos 'n' Andy,* in his view, focused unduly on that "rapidly decreasing" portion of the African American population, thereby allowing "the crude deeds of unfortunates to be paraded as the order and pattern of a whole people." Responding to defenders who pointed out that the word *nigger* was never heard on the show, the bishop suggested that blacks needed to cease being satisfied with merely the absence of the worst racial derogation.[85]

Robert L. Vann, the editor of the *Pittsburgh Courier,* also attacked *Amos 'n' Andy*. In 1931 he launched a drive to obtain one million signatures on a petition demanding that the

Federal Radio Commission ban the program. The petition complained that "two white men . . . have been exploiting certain types of American Negro for purely commercial gain" and that their representations "are of such character as to prove detrimental to the self-respect and general advancement of the Negro." More specifically, "Negro womanhood has been broadcast to the world as indulging in bigamy, lawyers as schemers and crooks and Negro Secret Orders as organizations where money is filched from . . . members by dishonest methods, thereby placing all these activities among Negroes in a most harmful and degrading light."[86] According to the *Courier*, 740,000 people eventually signed the petition.

A third important critic of *Amos 'n' Andy* was the NAACP. When the program switched over to television in 1951, the country's foremost guardian of black advancement vigorously objected. Until that point the organization had refrained from criticism, but according to the NAACP leadership, "The visual impact [of the television show makes it] infinitely worse than the radio version." Anticipating Bill Cosby's annoyance with *Def Comedy Jam,* NAACP officials asserted that *Amos 'n' Andy* "say[s] to millions of white Americans who know nothing about Negroes . . . that this is the way Negroes are."[87]

A thorough assessment of such critiques requires an acknowledgment of the plurality of tastes, aspirations, interests, and perspectives within African American communities.[88] While an appreciable number of blacks repudiated *Amos 'n' Andy,* many others enjoyed it, a fact memorialized in letters, newspaper accounts, and the racial demographics of the show's audience. Black support, moreover, extended beyond the ranks of ordinary folk, finding a foothold in institutions and among cadres of intellectuals and activists. Thus, even as the *Pittsburgh Courier* was railing against the white authors of *Amos 'n' Andy,* the Chicago *Defender,* the nation's leading black weekly newspaper, was designating them honored guests at a parade and picnic on that city's South Side. In 1930, a young black journalist who would eventually head the NAACP defended *Amos 'n' Andy* and criticized its critics. According to Roy Wilkins, black opponents of the show should stop "sniffing about with [their] heads in the clouds," put aside "false pride," and start producing some humor of their own that would earn a share of the hundreds of thousands of dollars that the white producers of *Amos 'n' Andy* were making. Wilkins saw nothing wrong with the portraiture generated by *Amos 'n' Andy*. How would critics wish to have the show's characters presented? he asked. "In plug hats, with morning coat, striped trousers, glassined hair, spats, patent leather shoes, and an Oxford accent? Instead of having them struggling with the immediate and universal problem of how to get and keep a decent and usable spare tire for the taxicab, would [the critics] have them prating about mergers, mortgages, international loans and foreign trade balances?" Praising its "universal appeal," Wilkins concluded that *Amos 'n' Andy* was "clean fun from beginning to end," with "all the pathos, humor, vanity, glory, problems and solutions that beset ordinary mortals."[89]

Wilkins's perspective was by no means idiosyncratic. A prominent black attorney in Worcester, Massachusetts, declared that he could discern no good objection to *Amos 'n'*

Andy; he found the show truly funny and dismissed the racial critique of the series as nothing more than the whining of blacks who were "thin-skinned" and "supersensitive."[90] Interpreting the show completely differently than its detractors, a black fan in Chicago maintained that *Amos 'n' Andy* showed that "the Negro race has and does . . . produce people who are worthwhile."[91] Theophilus Lewis, an acerbic black columnist for the *Amsterdam News,* suggested that the *Courier'*s petition campaign against the program would serve one good end: "When they complete their tally of signatures we will know precisely how many half-wits there are in the race."[92]

In the 1950s, when debate shifted to the fate of *Amos 'n' Andy* on television, black opinion remained divided, though its opponents had gained considerable ground. As head of the NAACP, Roy Wilkins switched sides and called for the show to be taken off the air. In adopting that position he was supported by, among others, Thurgood Marshall (who would later, as we have seen, become the first black Supreme Court justice) and William Hastie (who would be the first black to sit on a federal court of appeals). Nevertheless, as Bill Cosby recognized, many blacks continued to support the show. In an ad hoc "man in the street" survey conducted by the black *Journal and Guide* newspaper in Norfolk, Virginia, a large majority of blacks voiced approval of *Amos 'n' Andy*. A poll taken by an opinion-research firm hired by an advertiser found the same result: among 365 black adults contacted in New York and New Jersey, 70 percent expressed a favorable view of the program.[93]

Today's conflicts over *nigger* replicate yesterday's conflicts over *Amos 'n' Andy*. Among the supporters of that show were black entertainers who stood to make money and gain visibility by participating in its production. Among the supporters of *Def Comedy Jam* and other, similar programs of our own day are black performers hungry for a break; to them, Bill Cosby's militant aversion to the N-word as entertainment is an indulgence that they themselves are hardly in a position to afford. Black critics of the campaign against *Amos 'n' Andy* charged that the show's detractors were excessively concerned about white people's perceptions. Today a similar charge is leveled. Some entertainers who openly use *nigger* reject Cosby's politics of respectability, which counsels African Americans to mind their manners and mouths in the presence of whites. This group of performers doubts the efficacy of seeking to burnish the image of African Americans in the eyes of white folk. Some think that the racial perceptions of most whites are beyond changing; others believe that whatever marginal benefits a politics of respectability may yield are not worth the psychic cost of giving up or diluting cultural rituals that blacks enjoy. This latter attitude is effectively expressed by the remark "I don't give a fuck." These entertainers don't care whether whites find *nigger* upsetting. They don't care whether whites are confused by blacks' use of the term. And they don't care whether whites who hear blacks using the N-word think that African Americans lack self-respect. The black comedians and rappers who use and enjoy *nigger* care principally, perhaps exclusively, about what they *themselves* think, desire, and enjoy—which is part of their allure. Many people (including me) are drawn to these performers despite their many faults because, among other things, they exhibit a bracing independence. They eschew boring conventions, including the one that maintains, despite massive evidence to the contrary, that *nigger* can mean only one thing.

CHAPTER FOUR

How Are We Doing with *Nigger*?

lthough references to *nigger* continue to cause social eruptions, major institutions of American life are handling this combustible word about right. Where the most powerful and respected political and professional positions are at stake, public opinion has effectively stigmatized *nigger*-as-insult. Anyone with ambitions to occupy a high public post, for example, had better refrain from *ever* using *nigger* in any of its various senses, because the N-word rankles so many people so deeply. Political prudence counsels strict avoidance. We now know that a man can become president of the United States even if he is overheard calling someone an asshole, but the same is no longer true of a person who refers to another as a nigger: too many voters view such conduct as utterly disqualifying. It is precisely because seasoned politicians know better than ever to utter the word *nigger* publicly that mouths dropped open when, during a television appearance in March 2001, Senator Robert C. Byrd of West Virginia talked about having seen "a lot of white niggers in [his] time"—a remark for which he quickly apologized.[1]

Reinforcing public opinion is the coercive power of government as manifested in tort law and antidiscrimination statutes. As we have seen, in certain situations victims of racial harassment can obtain money damages and other relief from their tormentors or from employers who fail to address harassment that is brought to their attention.

Various forces prevent the complete eradication of *nigger*-as-insult. Some of these are negative, such as vestigial racism and toleration of it; in many settings it is still the case that a habit of using *nigger*-as-insult does not much hurt one's reputation. It is also true, however, that positive forces militate in favor of the survival of *nigger*-as-insult. One such is libertarianism in matters of linguistic expression. Protecting foul, disgusting, hateful, unpopular speech against governmental censorship is a great achievement of American political culture.

As a linguistic landmark, *nigger* is being renovated. Blacks use the term with novel ease to refer to other blacks, even in the presence of those who are not African American. Whites are increasingly referring to other whites as niggers, and indeed, the term both as an insult and as a sign of affection is being affixed to people of all sorts. In some settings, its usage is so routine as to have become virtually standard. *Nigger* as a harbinger of hatred, fear, contempt, and violence remains current, to be sure. But more than ever before, *nigger* also signals other meanings and generates other reactions, depending on the circumstances. This complexity has its costs. Miscues are bound to proliferate as speakers and audiences misjudge one another. The Latina singing star Jennifer Lopez said that she was surprised when some African Americans accused her of bigotry on account of lyrics in one of her songs that referred to *niggers*. Maybe she was merely posturing; controversy is often good for record sales. But maybe she was expressing genuine astonishment; after all, many African American female entertainers sing lyrics containing *nigger* without raising eyebrows. Perhaps a dual misunderstanding was at work, as Lopez mistook how she would be perceived and disappointed listeners mistook her sentiments.[2] The popular film *Rush Hour* spoofs this reality. In one of its scenes, a black character (played by Chris Tucker) is warmly received after saluting a black acquaintance as "my nigger," while a Chinese man (played by Jackie Chan) sparks fisticuffs when he innocently mimics Tucker's use of the N-word.[3]

A diminished ability to stigmatize the word is another cost. As *nigger* is more widely disseminated and its complexity is more widely appreciated, censuring its use—even its use as an insult—will become more difficult. The more aware judges and other officials become of the ambiguity surrounding *nigger,* the less likely they will be to automatically condemn the actions taken by whites who voice the N-word. This tendency will doubtless, in certain instances, lead to unfortunate results, as decision makers show undue solicitude toward racists who use the rhetoric of complexity to cover their misconduct.

Still, despite these costs, there is much to be gained by allowing people of all backgrounds to yank *nigger* away from white supremacists, to subvert its ugliest denotation, and to convert the N-word from a negative into a positive appellation. This process is already well under way, led in the main by African American innovators who are taming, civilizing, and transmuting "the filthiest, dirtiest, nastiest word in the English language." For bad and for good, *nigger* is thus destined to remain with us for many years to come—a reminder of the ironies and dilemmas, the tragedies and glories, of the American experience.

AFTERWORD

This book has been fortunate in receiving publicity that brought it to the attention of a broad audience. Prior to its release, David Kirkpatrick of the *New York Times* alerted the public to the unusual consternation and excitement that roiled the editorial and marketing departments of the book's publisher. After its release, Andy Rooney praised the book on *60 Minutes* and David E. Kelley featured it prominently in an episode of his prime-time television series *Boston Public*. The book has been widely reviewed in newspapers and magazines and attained bestseller status on a variety of lists. I feared that bookstores might hide or even refuse to carry the book because of its title. But that apprehension turned out to be largely misplaced. Although a few bookstores declined to carry it, most dealt with *Nigger* much as they do other books of serious nonfiction that sizable numbers of customers wish to purchase.

Popular interest in the book enabled me to travel around the United States to talk about it in libraries, bookstores, churches, colleges, and on radio and television stations. On one occasion, my host on a radio show told me right before going live on air that the station (WCHB-AM in Detroit) strictly forbade any mention of the word *nigger*. She informed me that I, too, would be expected to abide by that restriction. I thought for a moment of withdrawing; after all, under the station's rule I would be unable to state straightforwardly my book's title. But I decided to proceed. I am glad that I did, for my hour on Mildred Gaddis's "Inside Detroit" was thoroughly enjoyable. Despite the restriction, we discussed every major issue analyzed in the book. While I stayed within the station's rule by spelling out n-i-g-g-e-r or using the euphemism *N-word,* I also criticized the station's policy, noting that my self-conscious screening on air only stoked my desire to say the word out loud. Gaddis disagreed with much of what I had to say but did so with respect, grace, and intelligence, thereby making possible an intense but convivial and productive discussion.

In other places, too, I was delightfully hosted by harsh critics. At Howard University, the sponsors of my reading introduced the proceedings by making clear their objections to what I had written. Yet they noted what they perceived as certain virtues in the book, and declared that, in any event, whatever people ultimately concluded, the discussion should be conducted in a disciplined fashion. Again I was happy to be a participant. Criticisms were posed sharply and with fervor. People got agitated. But there was also laughter and give-and-take. I learned much and felt (and continue to feel) gratified that something I had written had served as the predicate for such a rich, instructive, and invigorating conversation.

In some quarters, however, my book and I received more than criticism. We received denunciation from those who portray my text as a deliberate act of racial betrayal. On radio programs I consistently encountered a few callers who, without reading the book themselves, urged listeners to burn it. During question-and-answer sessions after lectures, there were often a couple of people who would ask condemnatory questions—"Doesn't a Harvard Law professor have something better to do than write a book like this?"—and then turn their backs ostentatiously and depart as I tried to respond. A number of writers have penned tendentious attacks, castigating me as a "disingenuous," "idiotic," and obsequious Negro who merely tells white people what they want to hear.

The two features of the book that have attracted the most vociferous denunciations are first the title itself and second what some see as an egregious toleration for the intolerable.

As for the matter of the title, I must begin by noting that it is mine. I stress this fact because some journalists have reported that the title was concocted by the publisher. The lectures from which the book is derived, however, demonstrate my consistency on this point: all contain *nigger* in their titles. (See for example "Who Can Say Nigger? . . . and Other Related Questions" [The Tanner Lectures at Stanford, April 1999] noted on page 179.)

I put *nigger* in the title for several reasons. Doing so certainly apprises a reader of the subject of the volume; no one can accuse me of having failed to inform (warn?) readers up front about the topic of the enterprise. I also devised the title in the hope of spurring publicity and snagging the attention of potential readers. I thought that my provocative title might enable me to break through the layers of distraction that surround us all and win for my book at least a brief moment during which curiosity, perversion, or anger might prompt passersby to peek inside the covers of my slim volume. Although some detractors insinuate that there is something dirtying about that ambition, I do not consider it to be such. I suppose that I could have entitled my book "A Disquisition on the Etymology of a Word That Is Often Used as Racial Slur" or perhaps, more snappily, "A Study of the N-word," but those titles would certainly have been less memorable and eye-catching than the one I chose. At bottom, my defense is rather simple: I write books to be read. I therefore spend a considerable amount of time and energy figuring out ways to attract, keep, and persuade readers—a task that begins with the title.

Contrary to what some detractors suggest, *nigger* does not appear on the cover of my book absent a context for its presentation. The book's subtitle (a nod to C. Vann Woodward's *The Strange Career of Jim Crow*) immediately signals an intention to highlight the problematic status of the term—an intention that is advanced by over 100 pages of text, most of which focuses on the reprehensible ways in which Euro-Americans have deployed language to stigmatize African Americans. I show, as you have seen, that *nigger*-as-insult is not an inert linguistic fossil but remains alive today.

This point brings me to the second basis on which some have attempted to pillory me—the claim that I offer refuge to racists by defending black entertainers who use the N-word and, even worse (from their point of view), defending whites who use the term. There is some validity to this claim. By insisting that *nigger* does not signify only one thing—a term of racial abuse—and should not be forced to mean only that one thing, I necessarily open the door to uses of *nigger* about which people will disagree—a situation of ambiguity that some racists will probably exploit. But what is the alternative? An eradicationist response might decree the removal of all literature, without exception, from a school's curriculum that contains the term *nigger*. Such an action might well result in denying a literary refuge to bigots. But what about the book that you are reading at this very moment? Or what about the many classics of American culture that contain the word *nigger,* including Ralph Ellison's *Invisible Man,* Martin Luther King Jr.'s "Letter from a Birmingham Jail," or Richard Pryor's *That Nigger's Crazy.* Under the decree, you would lose the option of reading or listening to those works (at least while at school).

At a discussion in Louisville, Kentucky, (at the wonderful Hawley-Cooke Book Store), someone challenged my contention that *nigger* is an ambiguous term that can have a wide variety of meanings. She maintained that what I portray as complex is really rather simple. After all, she declared, everyone knows the meaning of *nigger* just like everyone knows the meaning of *bad*. Her example could not have been more apt—though it defeats rather than supports her point. In some contexts, *bad*—though typically meant to signify something negative—is used to signify something positive. When people refer to the incomparable singer James Brown as *bad* they are typically praising not condemning him. That is because many people (following a convention popularized by blacks) flip the meaning of *bad* in certain contexts, such that *bad* is intended to mean *good*. A similar process of flipping has occurred with *nigger*.

I deplore racist uses of any word. I believe that it is a good thing that *nigger* is widely seen as a presumptively objectionable term. I think that people who use *nigger* in their speech should bear the risk that listeners overhearing them will misunderstand their intentions. I am glad that many people who interview me about this book express discomfort with pronouncing the N-word (though I get the distinct impression that some of these protestations of innocence and discomfort are merely formulaic). *Nigger* has long been used as a weapon of abuse and continues to be so used today; we ought to be keenly attentive to that fact. The problem is that insofar as *nigger* is deployed for other, socially useful purposes—satire, comedy, social criticism—we should also be careful to make distinctions between various usages. Unwillingness to make distinctions—the upshot of the eradicationist approach—generates all too many pathetic episodes like the one that involved Ken Hardy, the (white) teacher who was fired from his job as an instructor at a public community college because he mentioned *nigger* in a class about (of all things!) tabooed expression.

One purpose of this book has been to urge caution before attributing the worst meaning and motives to any word or symbol since all can be put to a variety of purposes, good as well as bad. The swastika evokes memories of evils that are among the worst in all of world history. Yet artists (for example, Art Spiegelman and Steven Spielberg) have movingly used the swastika in a variety of useful ways, including comedic lampoons designed to satirize Hitler's colossal failure. Another purpose of my book has been to counsel likely targets of racist abuse to respond in ways that are self-empowering. All too often, they are told that they should become emotionally overwrought upon encountering racist taunts. They are taught that they ought to feel deeply wounded and that authorities should therefore protect them from this potentially crippling harm by prohibiting *nigger* and other such words and punishing transgressions severely. In my view, such a lesson cedes too much power to bigots who seek to draw psychological blood from their quarry. A better lesson to convey is that targets of abuse can themselves play significant roles in shaping the terrain of conflict and thus lessen their vulnerability through creative, intelligent, and supple reactions.

In the course of talking with readers of this book I have benefited from listening to people describe reactions to *nigger*-as-insult. One of my favorite anecdotes involves the distinguished black physician, Dr. Thaddeus Bell of Charleston, South Carolina, who recalls that several years ago at a hospital in the Deep South he found himself leading an all-white group of interns on rounds. Right in the middle of one of the interns' presentations, a white patient whom the group had thought was asleep suddenly bolted upright in his bed, looked directly at Dr. Bell, and declared loudly "I don't want no nigger doctor touching me." The room went still; one could hear the proverbial pin drop. Some physicians in Dr. Bell's shoes would have berated the patient or stormed out of the room. Dr. Bell, however, refused to permit the patient's outburst to throw him off-stride. He quickly and firmly ordered the man to lie down; announced (while winking at the interns) that he wouldn't let "a nigger doctor" near the patient, and proceeded to instruct the interns about the proper way to continue with the man's medical care.

The next day the patient begged Dr. Bell's pardon.

Finally, I would like to respond to the many readers who have asked me to explain the identity of The Board, the group to whom I dedicated this book. The Board consists of cousins who stay in close touch with one another and gather together periodically to mark signal moments in the history of their families. Although some members of The Board disagree with my conclusions, all have supported my efforts, a gift for which I am most grateful.

ENDNOTES

Introduction to the Twentieth-Anniversary Edition

1. See *Powell v. Kelly,* 562 F.3d 656 (4th Cir. 2009).

2. *United States v. Bartlett,* 567 F.3d 901 (7th Cir. 2009).

3. *Middlebrooks v. Bell,* 619 F.3d 526 (6th Cir. 2011).

4. *United States v. Houghtaling,* 390 Fed App'x. 604 (7th Cir. 2010). See also *United States v. White,* 698 F.3d 1005 (7th Cir. 2012).

5. *United States v. Porter,* 928 F.3d 947, 953 (10th Cir. 2019).

6. Shane Dixon Kavanaugh and Andrew Theen, "White Nationalist Views, Arrest of OSU Student Government Rep Spark Outrage," *Oregonian* (Portland, Ore.), January 30, 2019.

7. *Rodgers v. Western-Southern Life Ins. Co.,* 12 F.3d 668, 675 (7th Cir. 1993).

8. See *McDole v. City of Saginaw,* 471 Fed. App'x. 464 (6th Cir. 2012).

9. See *Berryman v. SuperValu Holdings,* 669 F.3d 714 (6th Cir. 2012) (Stranch, J., dissenting).

10. Ibid.

11. *Sayger v. Riceland Foods,* 735 F.3d 1025 (8th Cir. 2013). See also *Bennett v. Riceland Foods,* 721 F.3d 546 (8th Cir. 2013); *Barrett v. Whirlpool Corp.,* 556 F.3d 502 (6th Cir. 2009).

12. *Matusick v. Erie Cnty. Water Auth.,* 793 F.3d 51 (2nd Cir. 2014).

13. *Swinton v. Potomac Corp.,* 270 F.3d 794, 817 (9th Cir. 2001).

14. In an email he wrote, "I believe I did use the 'N' word in reference to the current occupant of the Whitehouse [*sic*]. For this, I do not apologize—he meets and exceeds my criteria as such." Wesley Lowery, "Ayotte, Shaheen Want Police Commissioner Who Called Obama the N-Word to Resign," *Washington Post,* May 19, 2014.

15. Rick Christie, "Christie Commentary: Thanks for the Apology Senator, Now Please Go," *Palm Beach Post,* April 23, 2017.

16. Elijah Anderson, *The Cosmopolitan Canopy: Race and Civility in Everyday Life* (2011), 253. See also Akirah Robinson, "My First Time Being Called the N-Word," Feminspire.com, June 28, 2013.

17. Lawrence Graham, "The Rules," *Princeton Alumni Weekly,* October 8, 2014.

18. "Open Letter to Emily Dexter," Scribd.com, December 13, 2019.

19. Meghan E. Irons, "Official's Use of N-Word in Class Discussion on Racial Language Plunges Cambridge into Controversy," *Boston Globe,* February 7, 2019.

20. See ibid.; Marc Levy, "Removed Video Includes Students Deploring Loss of Message amid 'N-Word' Controversy," *Cambridge Day,* May 13, 2019; Juliana Vandermark, "School Committee Member Emily Dexter Resigns," *Register Forum,* December 23, 2019. See also Randall Kennedy, "When 'the N-Word' Meets Public Education," *Boston Globe,* April 7, 2019.

21. See Colleen Flaherty, "Too Taboo for Class?," *Inside Higher Ed,* February 1, 2019.

22. Ibid.

23. Ibid.

24. See "Faculty Respond to Professor's Use of N-Word by Calling for Institutional Change Around Racial Justice," *Echo,* November 20, 2018.

25. See Randall Kennedy, "How a Dispute over the N-Word Became a Dispiriting Farce," *Chronicle of Higher Education,* February 8, 2019. See also Mila Koumpilova, "Minnesota Professor's Suspension Fuels Academic Freedom Debate," *Star Tribune,* March 30, 2019; Robert Benne, "The Augsburg Concession," *First Things,* May 2019.

26. James Baldwin, "The Creative Process," in *Creative America* (1962).

27. Alison Flood, "White Professor Investigated for Quoting James Baldwin's Use of N-Word," *Guardian,* August 15, 2019; Colleen Flaherty, "N-Word at the New School," *Inside Higher Ed,* August 7, 2019; Colleen Flaherty, "New School Drops N-Word Case," *Inside Higher Ed,* August 19, 2019.

28. See "Professor at Wake Forest University Apologizes for Reading the N-Word Aloud in Class," *Journal of Blacks in Higher Education* (2020); Debra Cassens Weiss, "Law Prof Sues over N-Word Suspension and Says Being White Led to Different Treatment," *ABA Journal,* August 10, 2020; Eugene Volokh, "The Law School Acknowledges That the Racial and Gender References on the Examination Were Deeply Offensive," *Reason,* January 15, 2021; Clarence Page, "Yes, There Is a Case for Using Offensive Words in Classrooms—in Certain Situations," *Philadelphia Tribune,* May 21, 2021; Nick Anderson, "A Stanford Law Professor Read a Quote with the N-Word to His Class, Stirring Outrage at the School," *Washington Post,* June 3, 2020. See generally Randall Kennedy and Eugene Volokh, "The New Taboo: Quoting Epithets in the Classroom and Beyond," *Capital University Law Review* 49, no. 1 (2021).

29. See Kennedy and Volokh, "New Taboo."

30. See Kathryn Rubino, "Law School N-Word Controversy Is More Complicated Than It Appears at First Glance," *Above the Law,* January 13, 2021.

31. Elie Mystal, "If One More White Person Tells Me About the Use-Mention Distinction to Justify Saying the N-Word, I'm Going to Vomit," *Above the Law,* August 30, 2018.

32. See, e.g., Alex Marshall, "Amanda Gorman's Poetry United

Critics. It's Dividing Translators," *New York Times,* March 26, 2021; Jan Breslauer, "Should Whites Direct Black Plays, and Vice Versa?," *Los Angeles Times,* August 30, 2009; Lauren Wissot, "Whose Story? Five Doc-Makers on (Avoiding) Extractive Filmmaking," International Documentary Association, September 28, 2017. See especially August Wilson, "The Ground on Which I Stand," *American Theatre,* June 20, 2016 (speech originally delivered on June 26, 1996).

33. See Kevin Merida, "Spike Lee, Holding Court: The Director Talks Movies, Hollywood, Basketball, and, Oh Yes, Controversy," *Washington Post,* May 1, 1998.

34. Dave Itzkoff, "Maher Apologizes for Use of Racial Slur on 'Real Time,'" *New York Times,* June 4, 2017.

35. Tamara Ikenberg, "What Freedom Looks Like in 2017," *Anchorage Daily News,* June 13, 2017.

36. Frank Scheck, "Critic's Notebook: Bill Maher Gets Taken to the Woodshed on His Own Show," *Hollywood Reporter,* June 10, 2017.

37. Itzkoff, "Maher Apologizes for Use of Racial Slur on 'Real Time.'"

38. Bill Maher, "Please Stop Apologizing," *New York Times,* March 22, 2012.

39. See *Burlington v. News Corp.,* 759 F.Supp. 2d 580 (E.D. Pa. 2010).

40. Ibid. at 584.

41. Ibid.

42. Ibid. at 593.

43. Ibid. at 596–97. See also *Smith v. Lockheed-Martin Corp.,* 644 F.3d 1321 (11th Cir. 2011).

44. *Johnson v. Strive E. Harlem Emp't. Grp.,* 990 F.Supp. 2d 435 (S.D.N.Y. 2014).

45. 728 F.3d 1263 (11th Cir. 2013).

46. Ibid. at 1267.

47. See, e.g., Tyrone C. Howard, "It's Time to Completely Ban the N-Word in Schools," *Education Week,* October 28, 2019 (Using

the N-word "has to stop, and schools can play a critical role in helping to eliminate the word from our lexicon."). See also Mike Wise,
"A Word That Should Be Silenced," *Washington Post,* November 22,
2013.

48. See David Waldstein, "Scrabble Tournaments Move Toward
Banning Racial and Ethnic Slurs," *New York Times,* July 10, 2020; Ste-
fan Fatsis, "The Word Nerd Reckoning," *Slate,* June 18, 2020.

49. See Michiko Kakutani, "Light Out, Huck, They Still Want to
Sivilize You," *New York Times,* January 6, 2011.

50. See Joseph Conrad, *The N-Word of the Narcissus* (1898; Word-
Bridge, 2009).

51. See Jarvis DeBerry, "Keeping a Hateful Word Inside a Dictionary," *New Orleans Times-Picayune,* June 23, 1998.

52. Randall Kennedy, *Nigger: The Strange Career of a Troublesome
Word* (2002), 139.

1. The Protean N-Word

1. See, e.g., *Ohio v. Howard,* 1995 Ohio App. LEXIS 750 (Ohio
Ct. App.) (man killed in altercation sparked by his calling the defen-
dant a nigger); *State v. Higginbotham,* 212 N.W.2d 881 (Minn. Sup.
Ct. 1973) (man killed after calling a woman a nigger lover); "Black
Judge Adds 35 Years to Robber's Sentence after Felon Made Racial
Slur," *Jet,* October 10, 1994; "School Superintendent in Nevada
under Fire for Using Word *Nigger,*" *Jet,* August 28, 2000; "White
Bishop Steps Down from Charity amid Controversy over Racial
Slur," *Jet,* April 21, 1997; "Jaguar Official Suspended after Using
Racial Slur," *Jet,* June 13, 1994.

2. On the etymology of *nigger,* see the *Random House Historical
Dictionary of American Slang,* ed. J. E. Lighter (1997), 2:657. See also
the *Oxford English Dictionary,* eds. J. A. Simpson and E. S. C. Weiner
(2d ed., 1989), 10:402–4; Geneva Smitherman, *Black Talk: Words and
Phrases from the 'Hood to the Amen Corner* (rev. ed., 2000), 210–13;
H. L. Mencken, *The American Language: An Inquiry into the Develop-*

ment of English in the United States, abridged with annotations and new material by Raven I. McDavid Jr., with the assistance of David W. Maurer (1979), 383–84; Hugh Rawson, *Wicked Words* (1989), 268–70.

3. See Rawson, *Wicked Words*, 268–70; Smitherman, *Black Talk*, 210–13.

4. The linguist Robin Tolmach Lakoff speculates that *nigger* became a slur when users of the term became aware that it was a mispronunciation of *Negro* and decided to continue using the mispronunciation to signal contempt—in much the same way that certain individuals choose to insult others by deliberately mispronouncing their names. Robin Tolmach Lakoff, "The N-Word: Still There, Still Ugly," *Newsday,* September 28, 1995. But see the *Random House Historical Dictionary of Slang,* 2:656, where this theory of mispronunciation is discounted.

5. Hosea Easton, *A Treatise on the Intellectual Character and Civil and Political Condition of the Colored People of the United States; and the Prejudice Exercised Towards Them* (1837), 40–41.

6. See Sam Dennison, *Scandalize My Name: Black Imagery in American Popular Music* (1982).

7. Rawson, *Wicked Words,* 268.

8. Kenneth Porter, "Racism in Children's Rhymes and Sayings, Central Kansas, 1910–1918," *Western Folklore* 24 (1965): 191.

9. The NAACP has registered Internet addresses that contain the word *nigger* in order to preempt their use by racists. Even so, there remains plenty of opportunity for mischief. An Internet search performed in July 2001 using *nigger* as the key word pulled up 241 Web sites. See Julie Salomon, "The Web as Home for Racism and Hate," *New York Times,* October 23, 2000; Michael Mechanic, "Prempting Cyberhate," *Mother Jones,* September 1999; Mark Leibovich, "A New Domain for Hate Speech: Civil Rights Groups Struggle to Buy Racist Web Addresses," *Washington Post*, December 15, 1999.

10. Quoted in Stephen Kantrowitz, *Ben Tillman and the Reconstruction of White Supremacy* (2000), 259.

11. Quoted ibid., 297.

12. Sandra Kathryn White, ed., *In Search of Democracy: The NAACP Writings of James Weldon Johnson, Walter White, and Roy Wilkins, 1920–1977* (1999), 43.

13. John Egerton, *Speak Now Against the Day: The Generation before the Civil Rights Movement in the South* (1994), 117.

14. T. Harry Williams, *Huey Long* (1978), 705–6.

15. William Anderson, *The Wild Man from Sugar Creek: The Political Career of Eugene Talmadge* (1975), 207. Talmadge is also reported to have said, "No niggah's good as a white man because the niggah's only a few shawt yea-ahs from cannibalism" (quoted in Rawson, *Wicked Words,* 269).

16. Neil R. McMillen, *Dark Journey: Black Mississippians in the Age of Jim Crow* (1989), 205.

17. Ibid, 204.

18. Quoted in Len Holt, *The Summer That Didn't End: The Story of the Mississippi Civil Rights Project of 1964* (1965; Da Capo Press ed., 1992), 311.

19. William O. Douglas, *The Court Years 1939–1975: The Autobiography of William O. Douglas* (1980), 15.

20. See David G. McCollough, *Truman* (1992), 576.

21. Robert A. Caro, *The Years of Lyndon Johnson: The Means of Ascent* (1990), 70.

22. See, e.g., Anthony Summers with Robbyn Swan, *The Arrogance of Power: The Secret World of Richard Nixon* (2000), 354; Seymour Hersh, *The Price of Power: Kissinger in the Nixon White House* (1983), 110–11; Hilton Als, "This Lonesome Place: Flannery O'Connor on Race and Religion in the Unreconstructed South," *The New Yorker,* Jan. 29, 2001; Ralph C. Wood, "Flannery O'Connor's Racial Morals and Manners," *The Christian Century,* Nov. 16, 1994.

23. Harriet Jacobs, *Incidents in the Life of a Slave Girl,* eds. Nellie Y. McKay and Frances Smith Foster (Norton critical ed. 2001), 34.

24. Frederick Douglass, *Narrative of the Life of Frederick Douglass, an American Slave, Written by Himself,* eds. William Andrews and William S. McFeeley (Norton critical ed. 1997), 29.

25. Richard Wright, *The Ethics of Living Jim Crow in Uncle Tom's Children* (1940; Harper Perennial ed., 1993), 4–5.

26. Ibid., 8.

27. Ibid., 12–13.

28. Kathryn Talalay, *Composition in Black and White: The Life of Philippa Schuyler* (1995), 67–68.

29. Quoted in Susan Spotts, "Benjamin Jefferson Davis" (unpublished paper on file at Harvard Law School), 15. Also see Charles H. Martin, *The Angelo Herndon Case and Southern Justice* (1976), 48; Benjamin J. Davis Jr., *In Defense of Negro Rights* (1950).

30. Lerone Bennett Jr., "Chronicles of Black Courage: The Little Rock Ten," *Ebony*, December 1997.

31. Ely Green, *Ely: An Autobiography* (1966), 13–17, 24. See also Leon Litwack, *Trouble in Mind: Black Southerners in the Age of Jim Crow* (1998), 20.

32. Martin B. Duberman, *Paul Robeson* (1988), 55.

33. *The Autobiography of Malcolm X* (1965), 30–37.

34. Arnold Rampersad, *Jackie Robinson: A Biography* (1997), 142.

35. Ibid., 172.

36. Carl T. Rowan, *South of Freedom* (1954), 125.

37. Dick Gregory with Robert Lipsyte, *nigger* (1964), 185–86. See also idem with James R. McGraw, *Up from Nigger* (1976).

38. Holt, 258.

39. William Plummer and Toby Kahn, "Street Talk," *People*, May 13, 1996.

40. Kenny Moore, "The 1968 Olympics: A Courageous Stand," *Sports Illustrated*, August 5, 1991.

41. Marc Appleman, "The Kid!," *Sports Illustrated for Kids*, July 1, 1995.

42. Gary Smith, "The Chosen," *Sports Illustrated*, December 23, 1996.

43. Audre Lorde, *Sister Outsider: Essays and Speeches* (1984), 72.

44. Branford Marsalis, interview, *Playboy*, December 1993.

45. Lonnae O'Neal Parker, "White Girl?," *Washington Post*, August 8, 1999.

46. "White Girl—The Dialogue Continues," *Seattle Times*, October 22, 1999.

47. Henry Aaron with Lonnie Wheeler, *I Had a Hammer: The Hank Aaron Story* (1991), 230–48.

48. Forrest G. Wood, *Black Scare: The Racist Response to Emancipation and Reconstruction* (1970), pl. 4, foll. p. 84.

49. Quoted in David Donald, *Charles Sumner*, pt. 2 (Da Capo Press ed., 1996), p. 49.

50. Ibid., 84.

51. David Halberstam, *The Children* (1998), 261.

52. *Lynch v. State*, 236 A.2d 45, 48 (Md. Ct. Spec. App. 1967).

53. See, e.g., *United States v. Pospisil*, 186 F.3d 1023 (8th Cir. 1999); *Clifton v. Mass. Bay Transp. Auth.*, 2000 Mass. Super. LEXIS 22; *Guillory v. Godfrey*, 134 Cal. App. 2d 628 (1955); *United States v. Smith*, 1998 U.S. App. LEXIS 16406 (4th Cir.); *United States v. Hartberger*, 148 F.3d 777 (7th Cir. 1998); *Ohio v. Faye*, 2000 Ohio App. LEXIS 1971; *Norris v. City of Anderson*, 1999 U.S. Dist. LEXIS 22612; *Black Voters v. McDonough*, 421 F.Supp. 165 (D. Mass. 1976); *Solomon v. Liberty County, Fla.*, 951 F.Supp. 1522 (E.D. Fla. 1997); *United States v. Lansdowne Swim Club*, 713 F.Supp. 785 (E.D. Pa. 1989); *People v. MacKenzie*, 34 Cal. App. 4th 1256 (1995); *State v. Palermo*, 765 So.2d 1139 (2000); *State v. Colella*, 690 A.2d 156 (N.J. Super. Ct. 1997); *Mancha v. Field Museum of Natural History*, 283 N.E.2d 899 (1972); *City of Minneapolis v. State of Minnesota*, 310 N.W.2d 485 (1981).

54. *Random House Historical Dictionary of American Slang*, 2:664–65; *DuFlambeau v. Stop Treaty Abuse*, 991 F.2d 1249 (7th Cir. 1993).

55. Farai Chideya, *The Color of Our Future* (1999), 9.

56. Andrew Hacker, *Two Nations: Black and White, Separate, Hostile, Unequal* (1992), 42.

57. *Monteiro v. Tempe Union High School District*, 158 F.3d 1022 (9th Cir. 1998). Also see *Random House Webster's College Dictionary* (2000), 894: "*Nigger* is now probably the most offensive word in English."

58. Margaret M. Russell, "Representing Race: Beyond 'Sellouts' and 'Race Cards': Black Attorneys and the Straitjacket of Legal Practice," *Michigan Law Review* 95 (1997): 765.

59. Letter to the editor, "End Hatred and Its Code Words," *Des Moines Register,* December 28, 1999.

60. Ian Buruma, "Joys of Victimhood," *New York Review of Books,* April 8, 1999.

61. Iris Chang, *The Rape of Nanking: The Forgotten Holocaust of World War II* (1997).

62. Larry Kramer, *Reports from the Holocaust: The Making of an AIDS Activist* (1989).

63. Toni Morrison, *Beloved* (1987), v. Also see Stanley Crouch's review of *Beloved* in the *New Republic,* October 19, 1987.

64. For useful commentary on this point, see Peter Novick, *The Holocaust in American Life* (1999); Samantha Power, "To Suffer by Comparison? Genocide and the Jewish Holocaust," *Daedalus* 128 (1999): 31.

65. Quoted in Joseph Boskin, *Rebellious Laughter* (1997), 161–62.

66. See, e.g., *Goldberg v. City of Philadelphia,* 1994 U.S. Dist. LEXIS 8969 (D.C.E.D. Pa. 1994) (kike); *Vigil v. City of Las Cruces,* 119 F.3d 871 (10th Cir. 1997) (wetback); *United States v. Piche,* 981 F.2d 706 (4th Cir. 1992) (gook); *Huckaby v. Moore,* 142 F.3d 233 (5th Cir. 1998) (honky).

67. See, e.g., *Gant v. Wallingford Bd. of Educ.,* 69 F.3d 669 (2d Cir. 1995); *United States v. Sowa,* 34 F.3d 447 (7th Cir. 1994); *United States v. Ramey,* 24 F.3d 602 (4th Cir. 1994); *United States v. Juvenile Male J.H.H.,* 22 F.3d 821 (8th Cir. 1994); *United States v. McInnis,* 976 F.2d 1226 (9th Cir. 1992). See also chapter two, ahead, *Nigger in Court.*

68. 80 U.S. 585 (1871). Also see Robert D. Goldstein, "*Blyew*: Variations on a Jurisdictional Theme," *Stanford Law Review* 41 (1988): 469.

69. 80 U.S. at 589.

70. *United States v. Montgomery,* 23 F.3d 1130 (7th Cir. 1994).

71. Lawrence W. Levine, *Black Culture and Black Consciousness: Afro-American Folk Thought from Slavery to Freedom* (1977), 309.

72. Ibid., 341.

73. Ibid., 344.

74. Ibid., 319.

75. Howard Bingham and Max Wallace, *Muhammed Ali's Greatest Fight: Cassius Clay vs. the United States of America* (2000), 119.

76. *A Testament of Hope: The Essential Writings and Speeches of Martin Luther King, Jr.,* ed. James M. Washington (1986), 293.

77. Clarence Major, *Dictionary of Afro-American Slang* (1970), 84.

78. Claude Brown, "The Language of Soul," *Esquire,* April 1968.

79. Jarvis DeBerry, "Keeping a Hateful Word Inside a Dictionary," *New Orleans Times-Picayune,* June 23, 1998.

80. For an excellent discussion about *nigger,* on which I have drawn, see Smitherman, *Black Talk,* 210–13.

81. Helen Jackson Lee, *Nigger in the Window* (1978), 27.

82. Levine, *Black Culture and Black Consciousness,* 328.

83. *The Essential Lenny Bruce,* ed. Joel Cohen (1967), 16.

84. On Richard Pryor, see Richard Pryor with Mike Gold, *Pryor Convictions and Other Life Sentences* (1995); John A. Williams and Dennis A. Williams, *If I Stop I'll Die: The Comedy and Tragedy of Richard Pryor* (1991); Jim Haskins, *Richard Pryor: A Man and His Madness* (1984); Jeff Rovin, *Richard Pryor: Black and Blue* (1983).

85. Mel Watkins, *On the Real Side* (1994), 550.

86. In the early 1980s Richard Pryor announced that he would no longer use the word *nigger.* Explaining that a three-week stay in Africa (mainly Kenya) had had a profound effect on him, Pryor later wrote (in prose that initially makes one wonder whether he is being facetious) that "the land had been timeless, the people majestic. I had seen and felt things impossible to experience any place else on Earth. I left enlightened. I also left regretting ever having uttered the word *nigger* onstage or off it. It was a wretched word. Its connotations weren't funny, even when people laughed. To this day I wish

I'd never said that word. I felt its lameness. It was misunderstood by people. They [didn't] get what I was talking about. Neither did I." (Pryor with Gold, *Pryor Convictions*, 175. Luckily Pryor's racial enlightenment was delayed until *after* he had produced *Bicentennial Nigger* (1976) and other comedy albums reflecting his genius.

87. In print, see Chris Rock, *Rock This!*, 17–19 (1997). In audio, listen to Chris Rock, *Roll with the New* (1997). To view the performance, see the video, Chris Rock, *Bring the Pain* (1996).

88. Coolio, "Gangsta's Paradise," *Gangsta's Paradise* (Tommy Boy, 1995).

89. Ice-T, "Straight up Nigga," *OG: Original Gangster* (Sire Records, 1991).

90. Ice Cube, "The Nigga Ya Love to Hate," in *Amerikkka's Most Wanted* (Priority Records, 1990).

91. Beanie Sigel, "Ride 4 My," *The Truth* (Island Def Jam Music Group, 2000).

92. Listen to 2pac, *2pacalypse Now* (Interscope, 1991).

93. Eldridge Cleaver, *Soul on Ice* (1968), 9.

94. Harlon Dalton, *Racial Healing* (1995), 169.

95. Daryl Cumbers Dance, *Shuckin' and Jivin': Folklore from Contemporary Black Americans* (1978), 77.

96. Ibid.

97. Abiodun Oyewole and Umar Bin Hassan with Kim Greene, *The Last Poets—On a Mission: Selected Poems and a History of the Last Poets* (1996), 6–63.

98. Ibid., 60.

99. See Michael Thomas Ford, *That's Mr. Faggot to You: Further Trials from My Queer Life* (1999); Michael Warner: *The Trouble with Normal: Sex, Politics and the Ethics of Queer Life* (1999); Eve Ensler, *The Vagina Monologues* (1998); Inga Muscio, *Cunt: A Declaration of Independence* (1998); Elizabeth Wurtzel, *Bitch: In Praise of Difficult Women* (1998); Jim Goad, *The Redneck Manifesto* (1997); *Dyke Life: From Growing Up to Growing Old, a Celebration of the Lesbian Experience* (Karla Jay, ed. 1996); Jonathan Eig, "This Woman Wants You to Call Her Bastard,"

Offspring, June/July 2000 (describing Marley Greiner, founder of Bastard Nation); Kathleen Bishop, "Cracker Day Fun for All," *Flagler–Palm Coast Community Times*, March 29, 2000.

100. Bruce A. Jacobs, *Race Manners: Navigating the Minefield Between Black and White Americans* (1999), 102.

101. See Robin D. G. Kelly, *Race Rebels: Culture, Politics, and the Black Working Class* (1994), 209–14.

102. John Lennon and Yoko Ono, *Some Time in New York City* (Apple Records, 1972)

103. Patti Smith, *Easter* (Arista Records, 1978).

104. Anthony DeCurtis, interview with Eminem, *Rolling Stone,* July 15, 2000.

105. Quoted in Kelly, *Race Rebels,* 209–10.

106. Michael Eric Dyson, "Nigger Gotta Stop," *The Source,* June 1999.

107. Quoted in Robert Dallek, *Flawed Giant: Lyndon Johnson and His Times, 1961–1973* (1998), 44.

108. See Emily Bernard, ed., *Remember Me to Harlem: The Letters of Langston Hughes and Carl Van Vechten, 1925–1964* (2001).

109. See Langston Hughes, *The Big Sea* (1940), 268. See also p. 161.

110. Pertinent here is the following story, an anecdote saved from oblivion by the great sociologist Erving Goffman:

> I was once admitted to a group of Negro boys of about my own age with whom I used to fish. When I first began to join them, they would carefully use the word *Negro* in my presence. Gradually, as we went fishing more and more often, they began to joke with each other in front of me and to call each other "nigger." . . . One day when we were swimming, a boy shoved me with mock violence and I said to him, "Don't give me that nigger talk."
> He replied, "You bastard," with a big grin.
> From that time on, we could all use the word *nigger* but the

old categories had totally changed. Never, as long as I live, will I forget the way my stomach felt after I used the word *nigger* without any reservation.

Erving Goffman, *Stigma: Notes on the Management of Spoiled Identity* (1963), 29 (quoting Ray Birdwhistell).

111. Susan Schmidt, "Senator Byrd Apologizes for Racial Remarks," *Washington Post*, March 5, 2001.

112. See John Hartigan: *Racial Situations: Class Predicaments of Whiteness in Detroit* (1999). Related is the increasing use of "wigger," a reference to so-called white niggers—whites who immerse themselves in and express themselves through cultural styles, gestures, and tastes that are generally identified as "black."

113. Ibid., 116.

114. Ibid.

115. Arthur K. Spears, *African-American Language Use: Ideology and So-Called Obscenity in African-American English: Structure, History and Use* (eds. Salikoko S. Mufwene, Jahn S. Rickford, Guy Bailey, and John Baugh, 1998), 241.

116. *Towne v. Eisner,* 245 U.S. 418, 425 (1918).

2. Nigger in Court

1. Stephen J. Whitfield, *A Death in the Delta: The Story of Emmett Till* (1988), 37–38.

2. See *Hance v. Zant,* 696 F.2d 940 (11th Cir. 1983), *cert. denied,* 463 U.S. 1210 (1994); 114 S.Ct. 1392 (1994) (denying application for stay of execution). See also Bob Herbert, "Mr. Hance's 'Perfect Punishment,' " *New York Times,* March 27, 1994; idem, "Jury Room Injustice," *New York Times,* March 30, 1994.

3. See Randall Kennedy, *Race, Crime, and the Law* (1997), 277–84.

4. In the middle of William Andrews's trial for murder, for example, a juror handed the bailiff a napkin on which was drawn a man on a gallows above the inscription "Hang the Niggers."

Whether a juror did the drawing and whether other jurors saw it are questions that remain unanswered, since courts declined even to order a hearing into the matter. Andrews was sentenced to death by firing squad; see *Andrews v. Shulsen,* 485 U.S. 919 (1988). See also *Callins v. Collins,* 998 F.2d 269, 277 (5th Cir. 1993) (issue involving a potential juror's reference to the defendant as a nigger).

5. Jeff Greenberg and Tom Pyszczynki, "The Effect of an Over-heard Ethnic Slur on Evaluations of the Target: How to Spread a Social Disease," *Journal of Experimental Social Psychology* 61 (1985), 21.

6. *United States v. H. Rap Brown,* 539 F.2d 467, 468 (5th Cir. 1976).

7. Ibid., 469–70.

8. See In re *Stanley Z. Goodfarb,* 880 P.2d 620 (1994).

9. See In re *Ferrara,* 582 N.W. 2d 817 (1998).

10. See "Disciplinary Proceeding in Relation to J. Kevin Mulroy," *New York Law Journal,* August 23, 1999, 8.

11. Ibid.

12. See Kennedy, *Race, Crime, and the Law,* 256–62.

13. *Collins v. State,* 100 Miss. 435, 440 (1911). The Mississippi Supreme Court reversed the conviction and ordered a new trial, declaring, "The appellant may be a bad Negro . . . yet he is entitled to go before the jury of the land untrammeled by voluntary epithets" (ibid.).

The term *white man's nigger* was once common among blacks. Now it is seldom heard. The defense counsel in *Collins* offered a useful elucidation of the phrase:

It has two meanings, one which endears the possessor of the name to the average white man who looks upon this class as willing and obedient servants, ready to execute any commission a white man may set, whether lawful or not, and to the better white men, it often carries with it an idea that a white man's nigger is loyal, peaceful and faithful to the last degree to white ideals and white control. The average white jury would take it for granted that the killing of a white man's nigger is a more serious crime than the killing of a plain, every-day black man.

Ibid., at 435, 436–37.

14. John Egerton, *Speak Now Against the Day: The Generation Before the Civil Rights Movement in the South* (1994), 369.

15. *Taylor v. State,* 50 Texas Criminal Reports 560, 561 (1907).

16. *James v. State,* 92 So. 909, 910 (Ala. Ct. App. 1922).

17. *Thornton v. State,* 451 S.W. 2d 898, 902 (Tex. Crim. App. 1970).

18. In re *Jerry L. Spivey, District Attorney,* 480 S.E. 2d 693 (1997).

19. This account of the incident is consistent with the account offered by the Supreme Court of North Carolina. See In re *Spivey,* at 695. Further details are provided in the transcript of the hearing presided over by the trial judge whose decision to remove District Attorney Spivey was reviewed by the Supreme Court. See In re *Spivey,* transcript volume 1, 32–34. Mr. Roger W. Smith, who represented Mr. Spivey, generously gave me a copy of the transcript, which is now available at the Harvard Law School Library. Mr. Asa L. Bell, who represented parties seeking the ouster of Mr. Spivey, also shared with me instructive material.

20. In re *Spivey,* transcript volume 2, 159–60.

21. Ibid., 161.

22. Ibid., 197.

23. 315 U.S. 568, 571–72 (1942).

24. In re *Spivey* at 699.

25. Ibid.

26. Wendy B. Reilly, "Fighting the Fighting Words Standard: A Call for Its Destruction," *Rutgers Law Review* 52 (2000): 947, 956. See also Kent Greenawalt, *Fighting Words: Individuals, Communities, and Liberties of Speech* (1995), 47–64.

27. Cf. Kathleen M. Sullivan, "The First Amendment Wars," *New Republic*, September 28, 1992, 40, in which the author complains that the fighting-words doctrine gives "more license to insult

Mother Teresa than Sean Penn just because she is not likely to throw a punch."

28. *United States v. Alexander,* 471 F.2d 923, 941 n.48 (D.C. Cir. 1973).

29. In re *Spivey,* at 699.

30. See Howard Kurtz, "The Shot Heard Round the Media: Bush's Off-Mike Crack Could Cut Both Ways," *Washington Post,* September 6, 2000; Rob Hiaasen, "The Truth? Adults Use Bad Words," *Baltimore Sun,* September 6, 2000.

31. See, e.g., John A. Goldsmith, *Colleagues: Richard B. Russell and His Apprentice, Lyndon B. Johnson* (1998).

32. Cf. *Rankin v. McPherson,* 483 U.S. 378 (1986).

33. In Richard Wright, *Eight Men* (1961).

34. *Fisher v. United States,* 328 U.S. 463 (1946). For a useful and detailed description of this case, see David M. Siegel, "Felix Frankfurter, Charles Hamilton Houston and the 'N-word': A Case Study in the Evolution of Judicial Attitudes towards Race," *Southern California Interdisciplinary Law Journal* 7 (1998): 317.

35. Quoted in Siegel, "Felix Frankfurter, Charles Hamilton Houston and the N-word," 360.

36. Quoted ibid., 361.

37. See *United States v. Alexander*, 471 F.2d 923 (D.C. Cir. 1972).

38. A similar strategy would later fail another black man, who would be convicted of attempted murder in 1990 after seriously injuring a coworker who had repeatedly called him "nigger." See *Ohio v. Hall,* 1992 Ohio App. LEXIS 3915.

39. See *Boyd v. United States*, 732 A.2d 854 (D.C. Ct. App. 1999).

40. 214 S.E. 2d 85 (1975).

41. Ibid. at 89.

42. See *State v. Tackett,* 8 N.C. 210 (1820).

43. Ibid., Id. at 217.

44. Among the works I have found useful on this question are Alan M. Dershowitz, *The Abuse Excuse and Other Cop-outs, Sob Stories, and Evasions of Responsibility* (1994); Victoria Nourse, "The New Normativity: The Abuse Excuse and the Resurgence of Judgment in

Criminal Law," *Stanford Law Review* 50 (1998): 1435; idem, "Passion's Progress: Modern Law Reform and the Provocation Defense," *Yale Law Journal* 106 (1997): 1331; Joshua Dressler, "When 'Heterosexual' Men Kill 'Homosexual' Men: Reflections on Provocation Law, Sexual Advances, and the 'Reasonable Man' Standard," *Journal of Criminal Law & Criminology* 85 (1995): 726; Ann M. Coughlin, "Excusing Women," *California Law Review* 82 (1994).

45. Charles Lawrence III, "If He Hollers Let Him Go: Regulating Racist Speech on Campus," *Duke Law Journal,* 1990, 452.

46. See Richard Delgado, "Words That Wound: A Tort Action for Racial Insults, Epithets and Name-Calling," *Harvard Civil Rights–Civil Liberties Law Review* 17 (1982): 133.

47. Coughlin, "Excusing Women," 4.

48. Ralph Ellison, *Shadow and Act* (1964), 111. Ellison seems to have been quite interested in the phenomenon of provocation. At the beginning of his best-known novel, for example, we encounter the following episode:

> One night I accidentally bumped into a man, and perhaps because of the near darkness he saw me and called me an insulting name. I sprang at him, seized his coat lapels and demanded that he apologize. He was a tall blond man, and as my face came close to his he looked insolently out of his blue eyes and cursed me, his breath hot in my face as he struggled. I pulled his chin down sharp upon the crown of my head, butting him as I had seen the West Indians do, and I felt his flesh tear and the blood gush out, and I yelled, "Apologize! Apologize!!" . . . And in my outrage I got out my knife and prepared to slit his throat . . . when it occurred to me that the man had not *seen* me. . . . I was both disgusted and ashamed. *Invisible Man* (1952), 4.

49. My main guide on this matter is Dressler, supra, note 44.

50. See generally Daniel Givelber, "The Right to Minimum Social Decency and the Limits of Evenhandedness: Intentional

Infliction of Emotional Distress by Outrageous Conduct," *Columbia Law Review* 82 (1982): 42.

51. See *Wilkinson v. Downton,* 2 Q.B.D. 57 (1897). According to William Prosser, *Wilkinson* was "the leading case which first broke through the shackles of the older law" (*Prosser on Torts* [1971], 60).

52. *Bielitski v. Obadick,* 61 Dom.L.Rep. 494 (1921). See also Prosser, *Prosser on Torts,* 61.

53. *Wilson v. Wilkins,* 181 Ark. 137 (1930). See also *Ruiz v. Bertolotti,* 236 N.Y.S. 2d 854 (1962).

54. *Moore v. Savage,* 359 S.W. 2d 95; 362 S.W. 2d 298.

55. 355 F.Supp. 206 (S.D. Fla. 1973).

56. 768 So. 2d 1198 (2000).

57. 355 F.Supp. at 208.

58. Ibid.

59. Ibid.

60. 768 So. 2d at 1199.

61. Ibid. at 1201.

62. Restatement (Second) of Torts, Section 46 (American Law Institute 1964).

63. Calvert Magruder, "Mental and Emotional Disturbance in the Law of Torts," *Harvard Law Review* 49 (1936): 1023, 1035.

64. 355 F.Supp. 206 at 211.

65. Ibid.

66. *Bradshaw v. Swagerty,* 563 P.2d 513 (1977).

67. *Irving v. J. L. Marsh,* 360 N.E. 2d 983 (1977).

68. *Dawson v. Zayre Department Stores,* 499 A.2d 648, 649 (1985).

69. *Jones v. City of Boston,* 738 F.Supp 604 (1990). See also *Caldor v. Bowden,* 625 A.2d 959 (1993).

70. *Lay v. Roux Labs.,* 379 So. 2d 451 (1980).

71. *Paige v. Youngstown Bd. of Educ.,* 1994 Ohio App LEXIS 5942 (1994).

72. See *Parker v. DPCE,* 1992 U.S. Dist. LEXIS 16921.

73. My rendition of the facts in this case is based on the court of appeals' decision in *Brown v. East Mississippi Elec. Power Ass'n,* 989 F.2d 858 (5th Cir. 1993), and the unpublished opinion of the trial court.

It is also based upon the parties' briefs, which Alison Steiner, counsel for the plaintiff, was kind enough to send me.

74. 989 F.2d at 861.

75. Ibid.

76. Ibid. at 862.

77. Ibid.

78. Ibid. at 861.

79. *Spriggs v. Diamond Auto Glass Co.*, 242 F.3d 179 (4th Cir. 2001).

80. Ibid. at 182.

81. See *Harris v. Forklift Sys., Inc.*, 510 U.S. 17 (1993).

82. Ibid. at 21.

83. Ibid.

84. 242 F.3d at 185 (quoting *Rodgers v. Western-Southern Life Ins. Co.*, 12 F.3d 668, 675 [7th Cir. 1993]).

85. Ibid.

86. *Bolden v. PRC, Inc.*, 43 F.3d 545 (10th Cir. 1994).

87. Ibid. at 551.

88. Ibid.

89. Ibid.

90. See Eric Schnapper, "Some of Them Still Don't Get It: Hostile Work Environment Litigation in the Lower Courts," *University of Chicago Legal Forum 1999*, 277. Some students of the hostile-workplace case law assert that courts tend to be more solicitous toward plaintiffs making racial-discrimination claims than toward those making gender-discrimination claims. See, e.g., Robert J. Gregory, "You Can Call Me a 'Bitch'—Just Don't Use the 'N-Word,' " *DePaul Law Review* 46 (1977): 741.

91. 116 F.3d at 631.

92. *Jackson v. Quanex Corp.*, 191 F.3d 647 (6th Cir. 1999).

93. Ibid. According to another version of the facts, the supervisor stated that the sludge was "ass deep to a tall nigger" (191 F.3d at 652).

94. Ibid. at 659.

95. Ibid. at 662.

96. Cf. Steven Hetcher, "Creating Safe Social Norms In A Dangerous World," *Southern California Law Review* 73 (1999): 1.

97. *United States v. Magleby,* 241 F.3d 1306, 1318 (10th Cir. 2001).

98. *United States v. Tocco,* 200 F.3d 401, 420 (6th Cir. 2000).

99. Ibid.

100. *Robinson v. Runyon,* 149 F.3d 507 (6th Cir. 1998). See also *Heno v. Sprint / United Management Co.,* 208 F.3d 847 (10th Cir. 2000).

101. *Brown v. City of Hialeah,* 30 F.3d 1433, 1434 (11th Cir. 1994).

102. Ibid. at 1436.

103. See, e.g., Alan M. Dershowitz, *Reasonable Doubts: The Criminal Justice System and the O. J. Simpson Case* (1997); Vincent Bugliosi, *Outrage: The Five Reasons Why O. J. Simpson Got Away with Murder* (1996); Jeffrey Toobin, *Run of His Life: The People v. O. J. Simpson* (1996).

104. 1995 WL 15923 at 21–24 (California Superior Court transcript, January 13, 1995).

105. Ibid. at 25.

106. *Ross v. Douglas County, Neb.,* 234 F.3d 391 (8th Cir. 2000).

107. *Preston v. Preston,* 627 N.Y.S. 2d 518 (1995).

108. *Lee v. the Superior Court of Ventura County,* 11 Cal. Rptr. 2d 763 (Cal. Ct. App. 1992). Actually, Lee petitioned to change his name to "Misteri Nigger" but stated that he intended for the *i* at the end of the first name to be silent (ibid.).

109. Ibid. at 764.

110. Ibid.

3. Pitfalls in Fighting *Nigger*

1. Leon F. Litwack, *Been in the Storm So Long* (1979), 59.

2. See Charles Miller, "Constitutional Law and the Rhetoric of Race," in Paul Finkelman, ed., *African Americans and the Law* (1992),

416; Mencken, *American Language,* 379; Irving Lewis Allen, "Sly Slurs: Mispronunciation and Decapitalization of Group Names," *Names* 36 (1988): 217.

3. See Aljean Harmetz, *On the Road to Tara* (1996), 144; Leonard J. Leff, "*Gone With the Wind* and Hollywood's Racial Politics," *Atlantic Monthly,* December 1995.

4. Hugh Rawson, *Wicked Words* (1989), 270.

5. At the same time, Secretary Udall changed all "Jap" references to "Japanese." See Mark Monmonier, *Drawing the Line: Tales of Maps and Cartocontroversy* (1995), 52. See also Lois Thomas, "What's in a Name," *In These Times,* October 20, 1997; Richard Willing, "Cripple Creek, Squaw Tits, and Other Mapmaking No-Nos," *Washington Magazine,* June 1996.

6. See *Hamilton v. Alabama,* 376 U.S. 650 (1964). See also Petition for Writ of Certiorari to the Supreme Court of Alabama, No-793 (filed January 29, 1964).

7. William Bradford Huie, *Three Lives for Mississippi* (1965), 35.

8. See Robert McFadden et al., *Outrage: The Story Behind the Tawana Brawley Hoax* (1990); Grand Jury of the Supreme Court, State of New York, County of Dutchess, Report of the Grand Jury and Related Documents Concerning the Tawana Brawley Investigation (1988).

9. See Kathryn K. Russell, *The Color of Crime: Racial Hoaxes, White Fear, Black Protectionism, Police Harassment, and Other Microaggressions* (1998), 157; James Merolla, "Newport Woman Reports Getting More Racist Messages: Tisha Anderson Says She Is Afraid to Leave Her Apartment after Receiving Telephone Threats and a Note," *Providence Journal-Bulletin,* November 16, 1995; "Anonymous Donor Offers Reward in Racist Threat; Police Report No New Leads on Slurs Scrawled on Walls and Steps of the Newport Green Apartment Complex," *Providence Journal-Bulletin,* November 14, 1995. For a glimpse of the wasted effort, damaging confusion, and hurtful recrimination generated by this episode, see Celeste Katz, "Newport NAACP Branch Meets over Racist Attacks; They Question the Newport Police's Efforts and Demand Further Action in the Case of

Tisha Anderson," *Providence Journal-Bulletin,* November 18, 1995. For a murky case that seems to have involved another racial hoax in Providence, see Marion Davis, "Charges against Clemente Dismissed; Garrick Clemente Was Accused of Hiring Someone to Paint a Racial Slur on His Front Door," *Providence Journal-Bulletin,* August 5, 1996.

10. Russell, *The Color of Crime,* 162; "Sentencing in False Report of Racism," *Seattle Times,* December 11, 1996.

11. Russell, *The Color of Crime,* 163; Caitlin Francke, "Hate-Crime 'Victim' Pleads Guilty; Tenant Painted Slurs in her Townhouse," *Baltimore Sun,* January 16, 1997; Ed Heard, "Support Pours in for Targets of Racial Graffiti; North Laurel Family Gets Donations, Encouragement," *Baltimore Sun,* April 26, 1996.

12. Peter Applebombe, "Woman's Claim of Racial Crime Is Called a Hoax," *New York Times,* June 1, 1990; see also Russell, *The Color of Crime,* 160.

13. Applebombe, "Woman's Claim of Racial Crime Is Called a Hoax."

14. See Debra Dickerson, "The Last Plantation: The 'Niggardly' Scandal Should Teach Whites to Watch Their Language and Blacks to Toughen Up," *Salon,* February 5, 1999.

15. Julianne Malveaux, "Of N-Words and Race Men," *Black Issues in Higher Education,* February 18, 1999. See also Roy Riley, "David Howard Is History Because of Indiscretion," *Washington Times,* February 26, 1999: "Mr. Howard is history because he was not bright enough . . . not to utter the word 'niggardly' in a city that is predominately black."

16. See, e.g., Jonathan Yardley, "Cool Words Can Influence, So Drop Them," *Newsday,* February 4, 1999; Steven Pinker, "Racist Language, Real and Imagined," *New York Times,* February 2, 1999.

17. Dickerson, "The Last Plantation."

18. Courtland Milloy, "Some Words Just Taste Unpleasant on the Tongue," *Washington Post,* January 31, 1999.

19. Sam Fullwood III, "D.C. Mayor Under Fire in War of Words over Word Use," *Los Angeles Times,* January 29, 1999.

20. Barry Saunders, "That D.C. Style: A Kinte Cloth Mantle of Oppression," *News and Observer* (Raleigh, North Carolina), February 6, 1999.

21. Tony Snow, "Linguistic Lynching over 'Niggardly,' " *Des Moines Register,* February 3, 1999. See also editorial, "Obsessing over the N-Word," *Hartford Courant,* February 3, 1999 ("Talk about the excesses of political correctness: last week, an assistant to Washington's new Mayor lost his job for being literate. . . . A person shouldn't lose his job because others misunderstood proper word usage"); Lynda Hill, "A Word, a Hairtrigger Racial Sensitivity, a Job Lost," *Christian Science Monitor,* February 3, 1999; Ken Hamblin, "PC Police Strike Again," *Denver Post,* February 2, 1999; Cynthia Tucker, "The Blacker-Than-Thou Thing," *Denver Post,* February 2, 1999.

22. See Gwen Carleton, " 'Niggardly' Upsets UW Student," *Capitol Times* (Madison, Wisconsin), February 2, 1999.

23. Natalie Anderson, letter to the editor, *Boston Magazine,* May 1998.

24. Sandra B. Fleishman, letter to the editor, *Boston Magazine,* May 1998.

25. Craig Unger, "A Letter from the Editor," *Boston Magazine,* May 1998.

26. See Lawrence Otis Graham, "Head Nigger in Charge: Roles That Black Professionals Play in the Corporate World," *Business and Society Review,* June 22, 1995.

27. See, e.g., Stan Simpson, "In Defining the N-word, Let Meaning Be Very Clear," *Hartford Courant,* November 3, 1997: "What would happen if a white friend were to come up to me and say [as does my black brother], 'Hey, Nigger! How are you doing?' Well, excuse my ebonics, but we be fightin'."

28. Listen to Chris Rock, "Niggers vs. Black People," on *Roll with the New* (1997). For the video performance, see Chris Rock, *Bring the Pain* (1996).

29. Quoted in Kathleen Pfeiffer, introduction to Carl Van Vech-

ten, *Nigger Heaven* (University of Illinois Press ed., 2000; orig. pub. 1926), xiv.

30. Quoted ibid.

31. Quoted ibid., xiv, xxx, xxxi.

32. Quoted ibid., xxx.

33. Quoted ibid., xxvii.

34. See Kevin Merida, "Spike Lee, Holding Court: The Director Talks Movies, Hollywood, Basketball and, Oh Yes, Controversy," *Washington Post,* May 1, 1998.

35. See Lynne K. Varner and Hugo Kugiya, "What's in a Name?—A Hated Racial Slur Finds New Currency—and Controversy—in Popular Culture," *Seattle Times,* July 6, 1998.

36. See Richard Corliss, "The Scheme of a Notion," *Time,* October 9, 2000; "Spike's Minstrel Show," *Newsweek,* October 2, 2000.

37. Delphine Abraham, "Changing Webster's Dictionary," *Essence,* March 1998.

38. Ibid.

39. "NAACP Leader Kweisi Mfume Says Merriam-Webster's Decision on Use of Racial Slurs Is 'Unacceptable,' " *Jet,* May 25, 1998.

40. See John M. Morse, "Sparing Sensitivities Isn't Dictionary's Job," *USA Today,* May 11, 1998.

41. Quoted in Jarvis DeBerry, "Keeping a Hateful Word inside a Dictionary," *New Orleans Times-Picayune,* June 23, 1998.

42. John H. Wallace, "The Case against *Huck Finn,*" in James S. Leonard, Thomas A. Tenney, and Thaddious M. Davis, eds., *Satire or Evasion: Black Perspectives on "Huckleberry Finn"* (1992), 16.

43. Mark Twain, *Adventures of Huckleberry Finn,* ed. Thomas Cooley, Norton critical ed., 3d ed. (1999).

44. Wallace, "The Case against *Huck Finn,*" 21.

45. See Shelley Fisher Fishkin, *Lighting Out for the Territory: Reflections on Mark Twain and American Culture* (1996), 73–74.

46. Quoted ibid., 82.

47. See, e.g., Jane Smiley, "Say It Ain't So, Huck: Second

Thoughts on Mark Twain's 'Masterpiece,' " in *Adventures of Huckleberry Finn,* Norton critical ed.

48. See *United States v. J.H.H.,* 22 F.3d 821 (8th Cir. 1994).

49. See *Dambrot v. Central Mich. Univ.,* 55 F.3d 1177 (6th Cir. 1995). See also Michael P. Pompeo, "Constitutional Law—First Amendment—Athletic Coach's Locker Room Speech Is Not Protected under First Amendment, Even Though University Policy Is Found Unconstitutional—*Dambrot v. Central Michigan University,* 55 F.3d 1177 (6th Cir. 1995)," *Seton Hall Journal of Sport Law* 6 (1996): 277. My understanding of *Dambrot* has also been enriched by conversations with Professor Robert A. Sedler, who represented Coach Dambrot on appeal.

50. See First Brief of Plaintiffs-Appellants–Cross-Appellees in *Dambrot v. Central Mich. Univ.* at 6 (quoting Complaint of Keith Dambrot).

51. Ibid. Coach Dambrot had also said on one occasion prior to the locker-room incident that his players should not be "niggers in the classroom." Questioned later about that comment, the coach explained that he had been trying to express his feeling that "you can't be aggressive, tough, hard-nosed in class, especially at a school like Central Michigan University where the faculty members don't understand a lot about black people or have many black people in class" (55 F.3rd at 1181).

52. First Brief of Plaintiffs-Appellants–Cross-Appelless, *Dambrot v. Central Mich. Univ.* at 10 n. 4.

53. Ibid. at 11–12 n. 7.

54. Ibid. at 12–13 n. 9.

55. Ibid. at 13 n. 11.

56. Other coaches have used *nigger* in the same way Dambrot did. For example, testifying on Dambrot's behalf, Adele Young, an African American basketball coach, explained that "a coach is around the players seven days a week, nine months of the year. The players are a part of the coach's family. A coach can pick up the players' language and speech patterns without being aware of a change. . . . My players, both African-American and White, use [*nigger*]

freely as I do in the coach setting. When used in this way, 'nigger' means a tough, hard player. Coach Dambrot understood the way players use 'nigger' and when he used it, he used it the very same way they did" (Ibid. at 9).

57. Chris Colin, "The N-Word," Salon.com, November 8, 1999; Alison Schneider, "To Many Adjunct Professors, Academic Freedom Is a Myth," December 10, 1999. See also *Hardy v. Jefferson Community College,* 2001 FED App.0267P (6th Cir. 2001).

58. See "Black Students Forgive Teacher's Mistaken Slur," *New York Times,* October 17, 1988.

59. See Richard Delgado, "Words That Wound: A Tort Action for Racial Insults, Epithets and Name-Calling," *Harvard Civil Rights–Civil Liberties Law Review* 17 (1982): 133; idem, "Campus Antiracism Rules: Constitutional Narratives in Collision," *Northwestern University Law Review* 85 (1991): 343; Charles Lawrence III, "If He Hollers Let Him Go: Regulating Racist Speech on Campus," *Duke Law Journal,* 1990, 431; Mari J. Matsuda, "Public Response to Racist Speech: Considering the Victim's Story," *Michigan Law Review* 187 (1989): 2320.

60. See, e.g., *UWM Post, Inc., v. Bd. of Regents,* 774 F.Supp. 1163 (E.D. Wis. 1991); *Doe v. Univ. of Michigan,* 721 F.Supp. 852 (E.D. Mich. 1989).

61. For examples of this rhetoric, see Lawrence, "If He Hollers Let Him Go," 434, 449; Matsuda, "Public Response to Racist Speech," 2370 ("Marked rise of racial harassment, hate speech, and racially motivated violence marks our entry into the 1990s"). Even fervent opponents of speech codes accede without sufficient questioning to their antagonists' portrayal of rising waves of campus racism; see, e.g., Nadine Strossen, "Regulating Racist Speech on Campus: A Modest Proposal?," *Duke Law Journal,* 1990, 484, 488. For useful commentary on this point, see James B. Jacobs and Kimberly Potter, *Hate Crimes: Criminal Law and Identity Politics* (1998), 45–64; Richard Bernstein, *The Dictatorship of Virtue* (1994), 183–215.

62. Lawrence, "If He Hollers Let Him Go," 433.

63. Ibid., 432.

64. Ibid., 433.

65. Ibid., 434.

66. Henry Louis Gates Jr., "War of Words: Critical Race Theory and the First Amendment," in *Speaking of Race, Speaking of Sex: Hate Speech, Civil Rights, and Civil Liberties* (1994), 42.

67. Lawrence, "If He Hollers Let Him Go," 451.

68. See S. Douglas Murray, "The Demise of Campus Speech Codes," *Western State University Law Review* 24 (1997): 247, 266 n. 158. See also Handoff, "Chilling Codes," *Washington Post*, March 25, 1995.

69. Lawrence, "If He Hollers Let Him Go," 448.

70. Gates, "War of Words," 47.

71. See Strossen, "Regulating Racist Speech on Campus," 484.

72. *West Virginia State Bd. of Educ. v. Barnette,* 319 U.S. 624, 642 (1943). See also *Chicago Police Dept. v. Mosey,* 406 U.S. 92, (1972) (Justice Marshall: "Above all else, the First Amendment means that government has no power to restrict expression because of its message, its ideas, its subject matter, or its content").

73. See William Lee Miller, *Arguing about Slavery: The Great Battle in the United States Congress* (1996); Harry Kalven Jr., *The Negro and the First Amendment* (1965); Michael Kent Curtis, "The Curious History of Attempts to Suppress Antislavery Speech, Press, and Petitions in 1835–37," *Northwestern University Law Review* 89 (1995): 785.

74. Delgado, "Words That Wound," 180. Note, though, that Delgado adds yet another complication: if *nigger* "was intended and understood as demeaning, minority plaintiffs could sue other members of the same or another minority group" (ibid.). He does not broach the question of whether it would be permissible under any circumstances—e.g., if done with affection—for a white person to call a black person "nigger."

75. Matsuda, "Public Response to Racist Speech," 2364.

76. Ibid.

77. Langston Hughes, *The Big Sea* (1940), 268.

78. Lucius Harper, managing editor of the Chicago *Defender,* observed in 1939 that *nigger* "is a common expression among the ordinary Negroes and is used frequently in conversation between them. It carries no odium or sting when used by themselves, but they object keenly to whites using it because it conveys the spirit of hate, discrimination and prejudice" (quoted in Mencken, *The American Language,* supplement 1, 626).

79. Halford H. Fairchild, "N-Word Should Be Odious from Anyone," *Los Angeles Times,* September 16, 1987.

80. Ron Nelson, "The Word 'Nigga' Is Only for Slaves and Sambo," *Journal of Blacks in Higher Education,* autumn 1998.

81. E. R. Shipp, "N-Word Just as Vile When Uttered by Blacks," *New York Daily News,* January 21, 1998. See also idem, "There's No Excuse for N-Word, Now or Ever," *New York Daily News,* March 11, 2001; Mary A. Mitchell, "N-Word OK for Blacks but Not for Whites?," *Chicago Sun-Times,* December 28, 1997.

82. Quoted in Laura A. Randolph, "Life after the *Cosby Show,*" *Ebony,* May 1994.

83. See Melvin Patrick Ely, *"The Adventures of Amos 'n' Andy": A Social History of an American Phenomenon* (1991).

84. Ibid., 9.

85. Ibid., 171–73.

86. Ibid., 173–74. See also the photograph following page 82.

87. Ibid., 215–16.

88. I have focused in the text that follows on black defenders of *Amos 'n' Andy,* but the show also had countless white fans and a number of white champions, some of whom were undoubtedly profoundly racist. In August 1931, the editor of the *Sterling City* (Texas) *New Record,* for example, denounced Negro critics of *Amos 'n' Andy* as "a lot of fool Niggers" and opined that the series brought out "nigger characteristics true to Nigger nature just as it is among the denizens of the colored race in large cities" (quoted in Ely, *"The Adventures of Amos 'n' Andy,"* 185).

89. Quoted ibid., 171.

90. Ibid., 181.

91. Quoted ibid., 182.
92. Quoted ibid.
93. Ibid., 222.

4. How Are We Doing with *Nigger*?

1. Susan Schmidt, "Sen. Byrd Apologizes for Racial Remarks," *Washington Post,* March 5, 2001.

2. See Annie Nakao, "N-Word Use Increasing, Not Without Protest; Use of the Racial Slur Among all Ethnicities Elicits a Variety of Emotions," *San Francisco Chronicle,* July 29, 2001.

3. For a biting critique of Tucker's humor, including his use of *nigger*, see Justin Driver, "The Mirth of a Nation: Black Comedy's Reactionary Hipness," *New Republic*, June 11, 2001.

ACKNOWLEDGMENTS

I would like to thank Gerhard Casper, who, during his tenure as president of Stanford University, invited me to give the Tanner Lectures at his great institution in the spring of 1999. Those lectures, "Who Can Say 'Nigger'? . . . and Other Related Questions," provided the initial impetus for this book. I would similarly like to thank Professor Richard McAdams, who made it possible for me to deliver "*Nigger!* As a Problem in the Law," the fall 2000 Davis C. Baum Lecture at the University of Illinois at Champaign School of Law.

Harvard Law School is a wonderful setting within which I have been privileged to work. Dean Robert C. Clark, an enthusiastic friend of scholarship, offers constant encouragement, while colleagues and students offer productive criticism. As always, the staff at the Harvard Law School Library provided invaluable assistance. Especially helpful were the reference librarians, Deanna Barmakian, Amy Brower, Joan Duckett, Michael Jimenez, Janet C. Katz, Josh Kantor, Naomi Ronen, and Terry L. Swanlund. Particularly noteworthy among Harvard Law School students and professors who have offered helpful comments are Eve Madison, Mathew Tollin, David Solet, Justin Driver, Zachary Price, Sapna Sadarangani, Richard Fallon, Duncan Kennedy, Todd Rakoff, Lloyd Weinreb, and David Wilkins.

Other colleagues who have given me much-appreciated encouragement, information, and advice include Yvedt Matory, Sanford Levinson, Kathleen Sullivan, Stephen Schulhofer, Joshua Dressler, Glenn C. Loury, Jennifer Hochschild, Fred Schauer, R. Richard Banks, Kevin Mumford, Richard Ford, George Packer, Anita Allen, Eric Foner, and Vicki Schultz.

Mr. Benjamin Sears carefully typed the manuscript and buoyed many a workday with his good cheer. Altie Karper managed the copyediting with her usual grace.

My literary agents, Andrew Wylie and Sarah Chalfant, and my editor, Erroll McDonald, teamed up to make sure that procrastination did not stall publication. I am grateful for their efforts on my behalf.

Finally, I want to acknowledge again the people to whom this book is dedicated, folks who have surrounded me with love throughout my life: the men and women who constitute the Spann Clan's Board, led by its Chairman for Life, Gary E. Bell.

INDEX

Aaron, Hank, 19–20
Abraham, Delphine, 105–8
academia, speech codes
adopted in, 118–125
Adamo, Phillip, xx–xxiv
Adventures of Huckleberry Finn
(Twain), xxxviii, 41–42,
108–11
Africa, Pryor's visit to, 159–60
African Americans, *see* blacks
AIDS, 23–24
Ali, Muhammad, 28
All God's Chillun (O'Neill),
41–42
Amos 'n' Andy (TV), 128–134
Amsterdam News, 133
Anderson, Elijah, xvi
Anderson, Natalie, 99

Anderson, Tisha, 93
Andrews, William, 162–63
And Then There Were None
(Christie), 91
antidiscrimination statutes, 47,
70–82, 137
accumulated totality of racist
acts in, 81–82
asymmetrical rule,
xxx–xxxvi
direct evidence under, 75
hostile workplace
environment under,
xi–xiv, xxxiv–xxxvii,
76–82, 83–84, 87
overenforcement of, 76
racial discrimination under,
70–76

Grateful acknowledgment is made to the following for permission to reprint previously published material.